Point of Inflection

Frameworks and Tools to Accelerate Team Results

George Bradt
& Jeff Scott

GHP Press

ISBN 9781096119555

210808

For general information about PrimeGenesis' other products and services,
please contact us at inquiries@primegenesis.com or +1-203-323-8501.

Acknowledgements

This book represents our best current thinking on accelerating transitions and has its roots in *First-Time Leader* written with Gillian Davis, in *The New Leader's 100-Day Action Plan* written with John Lawler, Jayme Check, and Jorge Pedraza, in *Onboarding*, written with Mary Vonnegut, and in *The Total Onboarding Program* written with Ed Bancroft. So, thank you Gillian, John, Jayme, Jorge, Mary, and Ed for your contributions.

Beyond them we must acknowledge the contributions of our past and current partners in PrimeGenesis. Their fingerprints are all over this book and all our books and articles as we all work these ideas every day.

We are indebted to PrimeGenesis' clients on several levels. We are the first to admit that we have learned as much from them as they have from us. We are blessed to have the opportunity to work with an extremely diverse group of clients. They run the gamut from multinational to small, public to private, for-profit to not-for-profit. Their leaders come from many industries, from almost every discipline imaginable, and from many parts of the world. With every client, we have learned something new. Clients inspire, challenge, and teach us on a daily basis, and for that we are grateful.

To Meg, who seems to greet every one of George's new initiatives - from businesses to books to musical plays and everything in between - with a bemused look of "*Oh no. Not again,*" and ends up supporting everything he does in a way to which no one else on the planet could begin to come close, and has turned his focus from what he can do himself to how he can contribute to others - abounding gratitude. **

To Sandy, who did a lot of heavy lifting raising a wonderful family while Jeff pursued business pivots as an operator for over 30 years. Expressing gratitude barely does justice to her work.

Point of Inflection - *Frameworks and Tools to Accelerate Team Results*

Note: The tools printed in this book and other tools are available in a customizable format at www.onboardingtools.com. (See the BRAVE Leadership page.) We will be regularly updating these tools and adding videos and additional material on that page to give you the benefit of our latest thinking.

Additional tools on the website include the following. Many of these are more tactical in nature. If you're leading a smaller organization, you'll need them yourself. If you're leading a larger organization, the people working for you will need them.

Tool 4.2	Writing Guidelines
Tool 4.3	Meeting Management
Tool 4.7	Interview Guide
Tool 4.8	Interview Debrief Form
Tool 4.9	Offer Closing Process
Tool 4.10	Announcement Cascade
Tool 4.11	Accommodation Checklist
Tool 4.12	Assimilation Checklist
Tool 4.12	New Leader Assimilation Session
Tool 4.13	Acceleration Checklist
Tool 4.14	Career Planning
Tool 4.16	SMARTER Goals
Tool 5.2	Negotiating
Tool 5.3	Purchase Funnel
Tool 5.4	Strategic Selling
Tool 5.6	Sr. Management Trip Planning
Tool 5.7b	Weekly Milestone Report
Tool 5.10	Onboarding Risk Assessment
Tool 5.10b	Onboarding Risk Calculator
Tool 5.13	Problem Solving Approach
Tool 5.14	Personal Branding

Point of Inflection: A time of significant change; a turning point.

"No one should be ashamed to admit they were wrong, which is but saying, in other words, that they are wiser today than they were yesterday." - Alexander Pope

This particular version of Point of Inflection includes our best current thinking. Much of it is wrong. But all of us will be wiser tomorrow together and change the way we think and act as appropriate.

Overview: Accelerating Results Through Points of Inflection

Deming: "Every system is perfectly designed to produce the results it gets." Intel's Andy Grove defined a point of inflection as "An event that changes the way we think and act." When that occurs – most likely a change in your environment (like a pandemic) or change in ambition – change your system to change your impact and effect, changing strategy, organization, and operations all together, in sync, all at the same time to avoid breaking the system as you accelerate results through a point of inflection.

Note this is different than an event that slows your progress, but does not require you to change the way you think and act. If your strategy continues to be right, pause; regroup; then, keep going as you were, when you can.

Whether your point of inflection hits organizationally, personally, or both, you should be excited about the possibilities – and concerned about the risks. 70% of transformations fail to deliver desired results.[1] 40% of leaders fail in their first 18 months in a new role.[2] This is why we wrote this book – to help jump-shift your own game, accelerate success, and mitigate risks all at the same time with Core Alignment and BRAVE Leadership:

Core Alignment:

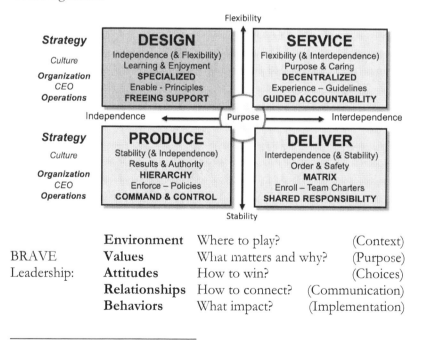

BRAVE Leadership:

	Environment	Where to play?	(Context)
	Values	What matters and why?	(Purpose)
	Attitudes	How to win?	(Choices)
	Relationships	How to connect?	(Communication)
	Behaviors	What impact?	(Implementation)

[1] Rajiv Chandran et al "ascending to the C-suite" McKinsey Insights, April 2015
[2] Anne Fisher, *New Job? Get a Head Start Now*, Fortune: February 17, 2012

Three premises:

1. **Points of inflection are defining moments**. Getting these transitions right and avoiding avoidable mistakes accelerates organization and personal impact, effect, and trajectory. If you don't think you're at a point of inflection, someone or something else somewhere else will inflect things for you. And you may not like how that story ends.
2. **Leading is different than managing**. Where managers organize/coordinate/tell, leaders inspire/enable/co-create. Be an other-focused leader, inspiring, enabling and empowering others to do their absolute best together to realize a meaningful and rewarding shared purpose.
3. **Leading requires choices** - and bold, decisive choices at points of inflection. Picking one over-arching strategy, aligned with one culture, organization, and way of operating seems riskier than keeping options open. But choosing to be superior at one thing versus good enough at many can be the difference between success and failure. Pick one.

This book provides foundational frameworks, insights, and tools to help by:

- Digging into the Core Alignment and BRAVE Leadership frameworks for leadership at both conceptual and practical levels. We combine them to guide what you should do next, later, never, and why; and how to accelerate impact and effect.

- Providing several lifetimes of leadership insights, examples, and stories from experienced leaders and experts to guide you through risk-filled situations you may not have experienced yourself – yet.

- Making available downloadable tools, easily adaptable for the situations you face. (Plus, bonus tools and new ideas over time, online at www.onboardingtools.com.)

Build Your Strategic Alignment and BRAVE Leadership from the Outside In:

1 *Environment*: Clarify Your Situation and Field of Play

Context matters. Part of your context is the choices the broader organization, community, or other stakeholders have made. If you've been assigned a particular sandbox, play in that sandbox. Part of your context is the rest of the world. Understanding your organization's history, recent results, and conditional changes and scenarios like pandemic curves are critical inputs framing your decisions. Choose to play where you can win.

- Understand the organization's history, recent results, changes and scenarios for business and competitive conditions.
- Align around an interpretation of the ever-evolving situation.
- Make choices around where to play and where not to play within your context to optimize your impact and effect.

2 *Values*: Align All Around the Organization's Mission, Vision, and Guiding Principles

Mission is generally given to you. You don't have a choice. On the other hand, you do get to choose your own picture of success - your vision. Guiding principles are the things you will not compromise on the way to delivering that mission and achieving that vision – values in action. Altogether, mission, vision, and guiding principles comprise purpose.

- Align on a shared purpose: mission (why,) vision (what,) guiding principles (how,) and any changes in your ambitions.

3 *Attitude*: Make Choices Around Overarching Strategy, Priorities, and Culture

Attitude is the pivot point. Align around one single overarching strategy to drive how you're going to win, along with strategic priorities, enablers and capabilities (win: predominant, superior, strong; not lose: above average, good enough; or not do/ally/outsource;) and make sure your culture is in sync with those (independent – stable – interdependent – flexible.)

- **Strategy**: The single overarching choice
- **Strategic priorities, enablers, and capabilities:** in line with that
- **Culture:** Behaviors, relationships, attitudes, values, environment

4 *Relationships*: The Heart of Leadership

You can't lead anyone unless you can connect with them. Connecting requires communication. And everything you do and don't do, everything you say and don't say, everything you listen to or observe and ignore communicates. Make conscious choices. Choose an organizing concept. MAP your communication message, amplifiers, and perseverance. The heart of leadership is the ability to build and organize an ADEPT team and make emotional, rational and inspirational connections.

- Be. Do. Say. Choose a cause that matters to you personally, live it, and then help others understand why it matters to you, how they should feel, the hard facts and your inspirational call to action.
- Organize as specializations, hierarchy, matrix or decentralized, potentially within a portfolio.
- Build an ADEPT team: acquiring, developing, encouraging, planning, and transitioning talent.

5 *Behaviors*: Getting Things Done

Environment, values, attitude, and relationships all inform behaviors and what impact you and your team make. It's all theoretical gibberish until you put it into focused action and follow through to ensure excellent execution.

- Focus on what creates the most value for internal and external customers, collaborators and stakeholders in your eco-system.
- Lead with a bias to freeing support, command and control, shared responsibilities, or guided accountability as appropriate.
- Track and manage priorities, programs, projects, and tasks quarterly, monthly, weekly and at least daily respectively.

Accelerating through strategic inflection points requires step-changes in strategy, organization, and operations, carefully synced together as outlined in the BRAVE Imperative Tool #1 below. Those are necessary, but not sufficient unless you reinvent yourself as what John Hillen and Mark Nevins describe in *What Happens Now?*[3] as a more sophisticated leader.

Hillen and Nevins argue that doing more of the same thing requires increased capacity or complexity while doing different things requires new capabilities or sophistication. If you're growing steadily, you can probably get away with evolving your mechanics, structure, processes, and systems with your technical and functional knowledge. But leading through a point of inflection requires new mindsets, capabilities, and behaviors leveraging political, personal, strategic, and interpersonal strengths.

Organizations go through predictable points of inflection as they outgrow systems, infrastructure, and their leaders. Many move through general, specialized, hierarchy, decentralized, and matrix organizations to portfolio management systems. A more sophisticated approach is to align your organization with your strategy as appropriate.

Similarly, some leaders fail to overcome stalls of poor story/narrative, alignment, influence, explaining and leading change, authority, focus, and leadership development. Hillen and Nevins suggest failing leaders add more complexity while more successful leaders add sophistication.

One aspect of that sophistication involves applying different mindsets at different times. Different situations require a leader who is chief enabler, enforcer, encourager, enroller, or the champion of customer experience.

---

[3] Adapted from George Bradt's May 15, 2018 Forbes.com article, "Reinventing the Missing Piece in Leading Through a Point of Inflection – You"

Putting this all together gets you to one of the four strategic frames. Note all organizations do all four, requiring the appropriate situational leadership. Your strategic frame choice yields a bias, not a sole focus.

Design-focused organizations need cultures of independence (& flexibility,) learning and empowerment. They should be specialized and led by chief enablers, leveraging principles and providing freeing support.

Production-focused organizations need cultures of stability (& independence,) results and authority. They should be hierarchical and led by chief enforcers, driving policies with a command and control approach.

Delivery-focused organizations need cultures of interdependence (& stability,) order and safety. They should be matrices and led by chief enrollers, leveraging team charters to push shared responsibility.

Service organizations need cultures of flexibility (& interdependence,) purpose and caring. They should be decentralized and led by chief experience officers, leveraging guidelines and guided accountability.

BRAVE Imperative

When people talk about getting everyone on the same page, this is that page. Everyone should be able to look at the BRAVE Imperative per Tool #1 below and understand the organization's direction under both normal circumstances and if you're leading through a point of inflection.

Start by thinking through a situation assessment, mission, vision, guiding principles, and strategic and business plan elements. Then flesh them out to clarify:

- Environmental insights and where play/problem to solve choices.

- Values including mission, vision, objectives, goals and guiding principles including the core nature of the business – what matters and why.

- Attitudes including the one overarching primary strategy, posture, strategic priorities, enablers, capabilities, and plans.

- Relationships including how your core team members will interact with each other and roll-out and ongoing communication plans.

- Behavioral tracking systems and management cadence: tasks – daily; projects – weekly; programs – monthly; priorities – quarterly; business and people strategy and operating plans – annually.

BRAVE IMPERATIVE

Environment – Where play/context
- Situation assessment combining insights around customers, collaborators, capabilities, competitors, and conditions, distilled into strengths, weaknesses, opportunities, and threats and
  - Key Leverage Points/Sustainable Competitive Advantage
  - Business Issues
- Where play choices

Values – What matters and why/purpose
- Mission: What called to do and why it matters
- Vision: What – Picture of success in which all can envision themselves
- Value Proposition: What's in it for them
- Objectives: Broadly defined, qualitative performance requirements
- Goals: The quantitative measures of the objectives that define success
- Values/Guiding Principles: That you will not compromise on the way – including core nature of the business (design, produce, deliver, service)

Attitude – How win/choices
- Strategic choices
  - Overarching primary strategy and posture
  - Priorities/enablers/capabilities (how win, not lose, not do)
- Cultural choices: Independent, stable, interdependent, flexible
- Plans: Direction/actions, resources, bounded authority, accountability: measures, milestones, who/how called to account

Relationships – How connect/communication
- Org. structure: Specialized, Hierarchy, Matrix, Decentralized
- Roll out/on-going communication (to those emotionally, directly & indirectly impacted – comply, contribute, commit - others)

Behaviors – What impact/implementation
- Ways of working: Freeing Support, Command & Control, Shared Responsibilities, Guided Accountability
- System to track, assess, adjust: task daily, projects weekly, programs monthly, priorities/processes quarterly/annually.
- Scorecard: Financial, Customer, Internal Business Processes, Learning & Growth

The BRAVE Imperative tool is the big cheat to this approach and this book. It's our core framework, laying out all the ingredients for success. The download of that tool and its instructions can get you 90% of the way to understanding our program. If that's all you need, download the tool, read the instructions, follow the steps below, and deliver better results faster. (Though you'll miss the valuable insights in the rest of the book.)

With all that in mind you can accelerate through a point of inflection by deploying five overlapping steps or building blocks differently in the different situations described in Part III of this book:

Assess & Plan	Strategy	Organization	Operations
Change catalysts:	Overarching strategy	Future capability plan	Leadership approach
Situation/ambitions	Strategic priorities	Immediate role sort	Management cadence
Best Current Thinking	Cultural changes	Leadership mindset	Incentives
	Ongoing purpose-driven **learning & communication**		

1. **Assess** the changes in your situation or ambition. *What* has changed? *So what* are the implications of that? *Now what* must you do? If the answer is nothing new, fine. But if the answer is to accelerate through an inflection point, put your best current thinking into a plan.

2. **Strategy.** Jump-shift your strategy, culture, and strategic process ahead of the point of inflection. Agree on a new overarching strategy, posture, strategic priorities, enabler, capabilities and culture. These are closely linked to your purpose, cementing the why of what you do.

3. **Organization.** Jump-shift your organization and organizational process. Create a new organizational structure and future capability plan in line with your new strategy. Do an immediate role sort. Accelerate individual transitions as appropriate. Deploy appropriate frameworks to help guide everyone's thinking.

4. **Operations.** Jump-shift your operations and operational process, implementing a new approach, flow, and management cadence to track and manage your priorities annually, programs monthly, and projects weekly as appropriate. Ensure your incentives reward desired actions and punish undesired actions.

5. **Learning and Communication.** Deploy a purpose-driven learning and communication effort in line with your new operating flow and management cadence. This is an ongoing effort, not a one-off event.

At every stage of working through an inflection, every single person in your organization and ecosystem will have one question that has to be answered before they can pay attention to anything else: "What does this mean for me?" Leverage your purpose, frameworks and incentives to reinforce all of that with a broader group over time systematically.

Call them what you want: moments of opportunity, moments of truth, moments of destiny. Whatever you call them, leadership and life is a series of them. Whether planned, unplanned, seen, unseen, known, or unknown, they come and go in a flash. This is especially true for points of inflection.

Leaders are defined by their followers. The only way to achieve your vision, in line with your values, in the context you choose, is through the attitude, relationships, and behaviors you model and engender in your followers. It's not about you. It's about your cause. It's not enough to have compliant followers, doing what they must. It's not even enough to have contributing followers. You need followers committed to a deserving cause. Be BRAVE yourself and inspire, enable and empower them to be BRAVE individually and together in a winning BRAVE culture.

One sign that you're scaling yourself is when you make the Time Management Flip and start thinking in terms of leverage, not efficiency. Flip the order. Do things to enable and empower others to do "their" work before you do "your" work. Make the strategic choices, creating and allocating resources. Bring out their others' self-confidence by giving trusted lieutenants direction, resources, bounded authority and accountability for results. Then, get out of the way. "Your" work will contract over time as you focus more on inspiring and enabling.

Throughout, our emphasis is on the application of frameworks and principles. This is a book and set of tools to be used and referenced, not something to be read through, considered, and put aside.

Note: The tools printed in this book are also available in a customizable format at www.onboardingtools.com along with extra tools for some of the chapters that we've moved to the web. (See BRAVE Leadership page.)

We will be updating these tools regularly and adding additional material on that page to give you the benefit of our best current thinking – which is better than yesterday's and not as good as tomorrow's, especially if you share your questions, insights, and suggestions with us at either gbradt@primegenesis.com, or jscott@primegenesis.com.

Part I - What is Your Point of Inflection?

"Sharon, you want to know what my problem is with Thomson Financial? Here it is."

Lacking in subtlety, Sharon Rowlands received this signal from one of her largest clients loud and clear. At the invitation of her client at Bankers Trust, she sat in a room with her client and 25 of her sales reps – all of which represented different products, had different business cards, and didn't know one another. This wasn't exactly the lesson that Sharon wanted to learn in her first days on the job leading Thomson Financial but it prompted a clear wake-up call, her business was in need of a point of inflection.

All businesses face points of inflection. That moment when you need to pivot is sometimes crystal clear yet other times it requires you to look beyond today's challenges and see what's ahead because not all of us get a brilliant moment of clarity presented to us like Rowlands. As a leader, you can get in front of it or you can wait for it to smack you across the face…but it's coming. How will you navigate that critical turning point in your business?

Andy Grove's Wisdom

Intel's Andy Grove is most often cited as the originator of this term 'strategic inflection point'. His remarkable career and success at Intel is well known. His wisdom shared over decades sheds light on his ability to navigate change and he described "strategic inflection points" as "…what happens to a business when a major change takes place in its competitive environment. A major change due to introduction of new technologies. A major change due to the introduction of a different regulatory environment. The major change can be simply a change in the customers' values, a change in what customers prefer. Almost always it hits the corporation in such a way that those of us in senior management are among the last ones to notice."[4]

---

[4] Andrew S. Grove, "Academy of Management, Annual Meeting", August 9, 1998

Grove is clear in stating that these inflection points are catalyzed by 'major' changes yet we live a world now where technology and media are creating a pace of change that is constantly unprecedented. As leaders, we must be cognizant of changes that are more pedestrian versus those that fall into the 'major' category but, for many industries, the major changes are more common than ever.

For example, if your business is in retail commerce, you've likely had the inflection point conversation because Amazon is the Darth Vader of massive strategic inflection points. Amazon has a direct impact on the behavior of all retail businesses but it also has become an *indirect* catalyst for smaller businesses as large retailers adapt their strategies to mitigate Amazon risk and target smaller industry niches and, thus, smaller businesses. The trickle-down effect of Amazon has created thousands and thousands of business inflection points on its own!

Grove tells us that an inflection point is "an event that changes the way we think and act." When that event occurs, most likely a change in your situation or ambition, you must change your system to change your results. This means changing your strategy, organization and operations all together, in sync, all at the same time to avoid breaking the system as you accelerate results through a point of inflection.

While 'major' is a common thread in Grove's inflection points, we should not limit ourselves to massive strategic inflection points. Massive changes – like the 1984 modified final judgment that broke off the Bell System or the introduction of the PC – are unmistakably 'major'. In reality for the rest of us, critical inflection points occur in most businesses every 5-10 years in competitive industries.

The S-Curve of business tells us that the process of growth for any business is fairly predictable and the cycles of business will bring most of us to points of stagnation where the growth curve flattens, or dips, and these challenging moments are the inflection points for us to tackle and create the next phase of growth for our companies. S-Curves are non-linear growth curves that commonly represent situations in business where revenue or market share for a product, or line of business, grows slowly at first, then grows quickly, and then decelerates to a slower growth rate. High-performing businesses work hard to smooth out that growth and find inflection points of new growth before the inevitable decline begins.

Products and businesses hit that point of diminishing returns in their lifecycles much more frequently than Grove's major events prompting an inflection. We've all been faced with growth challenges that lead us to pursue new customers, new markets, new products, new business lines, and generally new revenue. The goal is jump from a decelerating S-Curve to a new curve that promises continued growth rates. In their Harvard Business Review article, "Reinvent Your Business Before It's Too Late", authors Paul Nunes and Tom Breene speak to years of research that outlines how strategic growth isn't easy, but that it's a necessity for businesses to get ahead of their inflection points.

Nunes and Breene note that "sooner or later, all businesses, even the most successful, run out of room to grow. Faced with this unpleasant reality, they are compelled to reinvent themselves periodically." In fact, they go on to note research that, once a company runs up against a major stall in its business, it has less than a 10% chance of ever fully recovering. Those long odds explain why two-thirds of stalled companies are later acquired, taken private, or forced into bankruptcy.

As executives, we all believe that we have the power to fix things in our business that become broken but that misses a key point that Nunes and Breene make in their research. Their key observation is that business declines are usually not due to an inability to fix what's broken but, instead, are because companies *wait much too long before repairing the deteriorating bulwarks of the company*. In many cases for these companies that struggle, the recipe for change is a change in the leadership in an effort to infuse new energy and direction into the business. Continuity in your business performance requires change – don't be left on the sideline as your business evolves without you.

Grove's wisdom on strategic inflection points, coupled with the constant need for navigating change with the normal S-Curves of growth in our businesses, create numerous inflection points in our business lives. If we want to grow, we have no choice but to face up to the challenge.

Macro v. Micro Catalysts

Catalysts for your inflection points come in all shapes and sizes. The most visible of catalysts are those macro catalysts that impact hundreds of businesses, sometimes in dramatic fashion. That said, the most *frequent* catalysts are those of the micro variety which may affect only one company; but these catalysts can occur every few years (or more!)

Macro catalysts can be massive and they often build slowly when market forces create disruption. In the 1990s, the internet changed businesses globally over a matter of years as a tiny company called Netscape opened the internet for the world. Decades earlier, the introduction of the personal computer promised computing power on the desk – and eventually pockets – of consumers around the world to harness the power of technology. Only forty years later, it's difficult to imagine a world without personal computing devices, all of which were derived from this innovation that created a massive macro catalyst for change.

For many industries, macro change may come from other disruptions. The government is often the catalyst of macro change as regulatory changes can create impacts that range from increasing straightjackets for a business to creating such disruption that markets have to reinvent themselves. For example, the breakup of the Bell System, by consent decree, in the early 1980s created a new era of commercialism and competition for communications services that catalyzed inflection points across the industry.

The breakup of the Bell System was mandated in 1982 and went into effect on January 1, 1984. Its long-range impact has been profound but the change was met with equal parts opportunity and concern. Andrew Pollack in the New York Times wrote "A new era for American telecommunications and for American business begins today as the once-unified Bell System begins life as eight separate companies. It is a time of great expectations and great concern for both the telephone industry and the nation as a whole."[5] Yet the possibilities were clear as he went on to say "…The telephone system is, in effect, the highway system of the Information Age, and its health affects the competitiveness of all American industry. If the telephone breakup spurs innovation, it could help all industries."

As we know, the breakup sped the evolution of the communications industry – and many companies capitalized on the inflection point created by this massive change.

---

[5] "Bell System Breakup Opens Era of Great Expectations and Great Concern", New York Times, Andrew Pollack, January 1, 1984

Macro catalysts for change seem to announce themselves ahead of time and smart business people make plans to adapt well ahead of their moment of truth. On the other hand, micro catalysts can sneak up on a business. As Andy Grove said "…those of us in senior management are among the last ones to notice." Micro catalysts necessitate a constant vigilance and staying in tune with our customers – and our employees – so that we aren't caught off guard and find our businesses slipping behind.

Chances are, you are reading this book because a micro catalyst (or multiple) have started to impact your business. It may be that your competitor has released an innovative new product, it may be that your company has new owners with different expectations, it may be that your pricing is getting undermined in your industry, the list is almost endless.

Don't let your head be the one stuck in the sand. Action is better than inaction. As CEO of Netflix, Reed Hastings had it right when he said that "companies rarely die from moving too fast, and they frequently die from moving too slowly." We know what you're thinking, change sounds a lot better when it's somebody else having to change! Your situation may leave you with no choice.

The Practical Reality

By now it may be clear that the vast majority of us will face an inflection point for our business in the coming few years if we are in industries with any material competition. Whether you catalyze the change, or must navigate a strategic direction that's been handed to you, it will be your responsibility to make it happen.

When that time comes, your strategy, organization, and operations must all change…*in sync*…and at the same time. This book will create a map to help you tackle the most difficult challenge in executing on a synchronized strategy – leading people. The future of your organization may be at stake and it won't be easy.

The Odds Are Against Most People

You've seen the data about failed mergers before – up to 70% of M&A transactions fail to achieve the financial and strategic results expected of them[6]. Although you may not be considering acquisitions to drive your strategic inflection point, the truth is that the vast majority of strategic changes run the same failure risks because all of them rely upon a group of people rallying around a cause to make it work. It's to-may-to versus to-mah-to because acquisitions promise you new customers, new capabilities, and operational synergies yet most business inflection points strive for the same things…and they depend upon the same critical success factors. All of them rely upon people to execute. With acquisitions, you will rely upon people to combine businesses. With organic growth, you rely upon people to execute new initiatives and organizations. Unfortunately for us all, strategies that look right on paper can often not end well because a team of people are not aligned to get the job done. That's the root of the 70% failure rate and it likely applies to all inflection points in your business.

"Your organization's biggest challenge isn't strategic thinking – its strategic acting."[7] Peter Bregman rightly points out in his HBR paper that getting people to act on your strategic change is 10 times harder than coming up with the strategy in the first place. If you want to get results, your people need to be superbly aligned and laser focused on the actions that will drive the highest impact for your strategy.

I've got bad news for you, though. Only 8% of leaders are good at strategy *and* execution.[8] That's right, HBR says that 92% of you are doomed to be less than really effective at coming up with a proper strategy and then executing effectively. Chances are, there are multiple strategies that could be employed to find business success in your market so getting the strategy right is within your reach. When it comes to execution, though, there is likely one primary ingredient that is critical to your success…your effectiveness as the leader to rally a team toward strategic action.

How about a riddle to hammer home this point?

---

[6] Rajiv Chandran et al "ascending to the C-suite" McKinsey Insights, April 2015
[7] "Execution is a People Problem, Not a Strategy Problem", Harvard Business Review, Peter Bregman, January 4, 2017
[8] "Only 8% of Leaders Are Good at Both Strategy and Execution", Harvard Business Review, Paul Leinwand, Cesare Mainardi, and Art Kleiner, December 30, 2015.

Question: Five frogs are sitting on a log. Four decide to jump off. How many are left?

Answer: Five.

Why is that? Because there's a difference between deciding and doing.

In their book *Five Frogs on a Log: A CEO's Field Guide to Accelerating the Transition in Mergers, Acquisitions And Gut Wrenching Change,*[9] Mark L. Feldman and Michael F. Spratt of PriceWaterhouseCoopers provide insights for leaders in executing corporate change and capturing shareholder value. Read by many a CEO as they prepare to integrate acquisitions and deliver promised shareholder value, it equally applies to leaders that are navigating other changes in their business. As they state in the book, "Increasingly, the companies that win are those that learn faster, act quicker and adapt sooner. They will compress time by making and executing early, informed decisions about economic value creation, ruthless prioritization and focused resource allocation."

Feldman and Spratt have it right, the rapid pace at which you embrace change and rally execution of a plan will provide you a better chance of beating the odds and creating real value at your business.

Failures Abound

Let's get more of the bad news out of the way. For every transformational business success story, our data might suggest that there are nine or ten cases of businesses that missed their opportunity to pursue a new business pivot or failed to execute on a business strategy. Unfortunately, *failing to act* often leads us to the same outcome as *failing in action*.

Failing To Act

The pace at which hugely successful innovators can become obsolete is incredible in the business world of the past 30 years. It's hard to fathom that the giant inventor of digital photography could be close to obsolescence when their technology is omnipresent today but Kodak has (mis)managed just that. Equally unthinkable is that the most significant

---

[9] Five Frogs on a Log: A CEO's Field Guide to Accelerating the Transition in Mergers, Acquisitions And Gut Wrenching Change, Mark L. Feldman and Michael F. Spratt

early entrant in the personal device market – at 50% market share - could be out of the smartphone business within 10 years but that is exactly what Blackberry managed to do.

These companies wasted immense market opportunity because they failed to act in creating new inflection points for their business. Let's take a closer look at each to understand where they may have missed their opportunity for superiority.

Kodak: They Should Have Seen This Coming

Eastman Kodak was founded in 1888 and for most of the 20th century dominated the market for photographic film. Kodak was synonymous with photography as consumers everywhere tried to capture their "Kodak Moment." Innovation was a hallmark of the company and it invented the first digital camera in 1975.

In a cruel twist of fate, digital photography became the downfall of the company that was synonymous with photography and Kodak collapsed from a $30B market cap company to bankruptcy in a matter of decades.

Vince Barabba, a former Kodak executive, wrote in his book, *The Decision Loom: A Design for Interactive Decision-Making in Organizations,* of the catastrophic strategic failure at the company as it tried to protect its lucrative film-based business.[10] The Kodak engineer who invented the first digital camera, Steve Sasson, characterized the initial corporate response to his invention in this way:

"But it was filmless photography, so management's reaction was, 'that's cute – but don't tell anyone about it."[11]

Barabba recounts in his book that, with support from Kodak's CEO, he conducted extensive research to respond to the concerns of one of Kodak's largest retail photo finishers as they expressed concern about the advent of the first electronic camera from Sony. The research produced good news and bad news. The bad news was that digital photography had the potential to replace Kodak's established film-based business. The good news was that it would take some time for that to occur and that Kodak had *roughly ten years* to prepare for the transition.

---

[10] *"The Decision Loom: A Design for Interactive Decision-Making in Organizations,"*, Vince Barabba
[11] "At Kodak, Some Old Things Are New Again", Claudia Deutsch, New York Times, May 2, 2008

The problem, though, is that Kodak did little in this 10-year window to prepare for the disruption created by digital photography. While George Eastman, its founder, twice avoided disruptive innovations – once in moving the dry plate business to film and once when he invested in color film over black and white – the Eastman Kodak of the late twentieth century failed to adapt to pending change.

Kodak chose to use digital photography as a reinforcement for its film business and spent $500M to develop the Advantix Preview film and camera system to use the new technology but to protect its legacy. The new camera utilized digital photography as a means to preview pictures for printing – their bread and butter. The investment failed and Kodak eventually filed for bankruptcy protection in 2012. The digital camera killed Kodak, the very company that invented digital photography, yet sadly failed to act on it.

Blackberry: Myopic at The Moment Of Fame

In 2009, BlackBerry (then Research in Motion) was named by Fortune magazine as the fastest growing company in the world. As noted in TIME magazine, "the device was so ubiquitous on Wall Street and Capitol Hill that it earned the nickname 'CrackBerry'"[12]. Its devices were first introduced in 1999 and became a necessity for email-obsessed corporate professionals as it pushed emails to their pockets, rather than desktops. At its peak, BlackBerry sold over 50 million devices a year and owned over 50% of the U.S. and 20% of the global smartphone market.

Fast forward less than a decade and Blackberry is out of the smartphone business and its company value is a very small fraction of its former self. Apple's iPhone and Google's Android now dominate the market. But could this have been played differently by Blackberry? Their decline is a case study in failing to act – in this case failing to continue to innovate – in a market that is evolving quickly.

---

[12] 'The Fatal Mistake That Doomed BlackBerry", Sam Gustin, Time Magazine, September 24, 2013

There are multiple reasons for their precipitous decline but prominent theories point to a lack of foresight and vision to act on dominant trends in consumer behavior. For starters, BlackBerry failed to see that consumers – not business customers – would drive the smartphone revolution. Second, BlackBerry was blindsided by the emergence of the "app economy." Third, BlackBerry failed to realize that smartphones would evolve beyond mere communication devices to become full-fledged mobile entertainment hubs.[9]

Apple and Google had different visions for these handheld computing devices and they were clearly right. In late 2016 when BlackBerry announced that they would stop making phones, their dominant market share had shrunk to 0.3%. A sad tale for a company that had the opportunity to own a major share of how all consumers' daily lives are managed, yet failed to act on their point of inflection.

Failing In Action

The notable examples of companies that failed to act highlights how market leaders can fall quickly if they don't watch for changes in their environment and create inflection points to adapt. Failing to act, though, is not the only scenario in which market leaders can become case studies for things going wrong – many market innovators have soared before falling on hard times due to their inability to successfully execute in the face of change.

Blockbuster: Why Didn't They Stop NetFlix Sooner?

For anyone old enough to remember videos dropping into their VCRs to watch movies, Blockbuster was a juggernaut. The lengthy ritual of touring the entire video store for movie options that had yet to be 'checked out', was replayed over and over again. And after you had finished watching your video tapes, the last thing you wanted to do was ruin the economics of your rental by incurring the infamous 'late fees' by missing your return date. By the early 2000s, Blockbuster had grown to $6B in revenue and dominated the home entertainment industry.

Blockbuster went bankrupt in 2010.

What happened? NetFlix happened to Blockbuster in haymaker fashion. NetFlix was not a sudden foe, though. In fact, NetFlix proposed a deal to Blockbuster that could have changed the future of these companies in home entertainment but was rebuked. In 2000, the aforementioned Reed Hastings, founder of a fledgling company called Netflix, flew to Dallas to propose a partnership to Blockbuster CEO John Antioco and his team. The idea was that Netflix would run Blockbuster's brand online and Antioco's firm would promote Netflix in its stores. Hastings got laughed out of the room.[13] While Blockbuster went bankrupt within 10 years of that proposal, NetFlix went on to soar to valuations over $100B.

The fall from grace was dramatic but Antioco's actions may have been repeated by many of us if we had the dominant retail locations, brand, and customers that Blockbuster possessed in 2000. By taking an approach without storefronts, NetFlix had a lower cost base and could afford a different approach to rentals. It offered subscriptions and allowed their consumers to watch a video for as long as they wanted. What's that you say – no late fees? By the time of their meeting, Blockbuster's profits were highly dependent on penalizing their customers with late fees and the disruptive approach from NetFlix had the potential to prove painful.

Truth be told, Antioco did get Blockbuster moving in the right direction. They made changes in the supply chain with the movie industry to increase the availability of video tapes in stores, they eliminated the hated late fees from their model (at the expense of $400m of revenue,) and they were making strong progress in streaming video themselves. They peaked in 2004 on the back of strong business decisions by Antioco but the tide turned quickly after that.

The advent of DVDs started to make the mail rental business at NetFlix easier and they began to make ground. Between NetFlix and the internet, in general, Antioco saw where the industry was moving and made moves to adapt. One major move was a large investment in their digital platform, Total Access, which launched in 2006 and became successful very quickly (around 2m subscribers within a year). Total Access used a similar model to Netflix yet allowed customers to take the DVDs back to a Blockbuster store, rather than wait for postal mail for their DVDs. The ubiquity of stores created immediate gratification for movie buffs and Blockbuster was

---

[13] "A Look Back At Why Blockbuster Really Failed And Why It Didn't Have To", Greg Satell, Forbes Magazine, September 5, 2014

having an impact on NetFlix – so much so that Hastings asked Blockbuster to acquire his company in 2007.

What happened then? Execution stumbled at that point. Blockbuster had an activist investor, Carl Icahn, who had gained control of the board and did not like the direction that Antioco was taking. Antioco's demise led to a new CEO, John Keyes, who immediately reversed Antioco's changes in order to enhance near-term profitability, including cuts in spending to the Total Access program. Total Access stagnated and Keyes turned Blockbuster toward retail, one-stop shops for entertainment in a strategy that had failed once…and failed again. When video streaming started to explode, the show was over for Blockbuster.

Antioco deserves credit for acting but the failure of Blockbuster management to execute his plan led to the demise of the most prominent source of home entertainment at the start of this century. And led to the dramatic growth of the new home entertainment giant, NetFlix.

Netscape: They Should Have Known Better

As you know by now, Netscape created the first commercial web browsers and its founders invented the way by which most people on laptops and desktops interact with businesses online. They had first mover advantage and a sparkling persona when they IPO'd and sent public markets into crazed buying of this young company's stock. Of course, Microsoft was the sleeping giant and they woke up to the internet, and the threat of Netscape, pretty quickly. Was Netscape doomed at that point or did they have options to compete? Evidence would suggest the latter.

Faced with Microsoft as a competitor, Netscape had the opportunity to focus its strategy and fight back against the 800-lb. gorilla. Marc Andreessen created that opportunity by moving Netscape browser code to the open source development model and by selling the company to another major player in the personal computing industry, AOL. AOL had enough market share of US consumers to give the Netscape browser a chance to maintain market share in the face of Microsoft. But, things didn't quite work out that way.

Netscape could have honed its focus on sharpening their browser advantages and ensuring widespread adoption under the AOL umbrella but it chose a different path. As John Gable, former lead product manager for Netscape Navigator, noted that a focus on the browser development "would have bought us the time for our fantastic technologies to mature and bypass Microsoft. Instead, we tried to rewrite the entire Communicator Suite (including Navigator, email and Composer, all needed for enterprises – Microsoft's turf) and stressed new, not-ready-for-prime-time technologies over stability and compatibility that was essential for AOL to adopt Navigator. It took too long and didn't work that well."[14]

Meanwhile, the AOL acquisition of Netscape was also falling victim to the 70% failure rate for acquisitions. Within 18 months, key executives and engineers had cashed in on their equity and left the company and the battle for browser superiority with Microsoft was essentially over. Whether due to culture issues, poor engineering execution, or strategy missteps, the pioneer of the consumer use of the internet was relegated to a minor part of AOL's enterprise and the battle was lost. At their moment of truth, Netscape and AOL missed their opportunity to create an inflection point for their business with the modern browser.

MySpace: Corporate Greed Trumped by Customer Focus

Millennials will be the last generation that even know what MySpace was. MySpace was Facebook before Mark Zuckerberg and his company took command of the social networking space that MySpace largely created. Founded in 2003, MySpace gained a very fast following and was the top social network in the country just about the time that News Corp bought the high-flyer for $580 million in 2005. A few years later, Facebook overtook MySpace and never looked back.

Facebook grabbed leadership of the market in April 2008 and, in the three years following that event, MySpace lost over forty million unique visitors per month, lost both of its co-founders, laid off the vast majority of its staff and faded into the background of social media history.[15] News Corp eventually sold the business at a huge loss – for only $35m. The deterioration of $500m of value happened quickly, all at the hands of Facebook.

[14] "Why Did Netscape Lose Market Share?", John Gable, Forbes Magazine, November 25, 2013.
[15] "MySpace Collapse: How The Social Network Fell Apart", Amy Lee, Huffington Post, June 30, 2011.

In an interview with Businessweek, former founder Chris DeWolfe blamed MySpace's over-enthusiasm and under-execution on the product side for many of the site's problems. "We tried to create every feature in the world and said, "O.K., we can do it, why should we let a third party do it?" Rather than focus on a small number of key features, MySpace unleashed a slew of products that were buggy and dysfunctional.[16]

Meanwhile, Facebook started to let third-party developers create apps on the site in 2007 and had a lengthy head start on MySpace's decision to finally do the same. Facebook proceeded to create an ecosystem of apps – including wildly successful social games like Farmville – that became insurmountable. And, while Facebook's financial backers allowed it to focus on growing the community and usage, MySpace began to feel the pressure to drive revenue. This pressure not only clouded the focus of product development, it led to ads cluttering the user experience and becoming an irritant for its remaining users.

The story didn't end well. The MySpace founders left in 2009, and their successor left within a year after that, and the battle had been lost to Facebook. Critical junctures in their history created opportunity for MySpace to be at least as popular as Facebook, but poor execution led to its rapid demise. It stands as another casualty of a business that made the wrong moves in a rapidly moving environment.

Three Core Premises for Leading Through Your Point of Inflection

Don't buy in to the notion that 92% of leaders will be less than "very effective" in setting strategy and executing effectively. Instead, let's follow the lead of Jamie Dimon, the successful CEO of JP Morgan Chase, who says "I'd rather have first-rate execution and second-rate strategy any time than a brilliant idea and mediocre management." Multiples strategic approaches can work but leadership and execution are pre-requisites to success. If you're faced with a point of inflection in your business, your time to lead is now. The three core premises for your leadership in this moment:

1.   Points of inflection are defining moments

The great Herb Brooks, coach of the US Olympic hockey team in 1980, told us that "great moments are born from great opportunity." Brooks and his team became famous for conquering of the juggernaut Soviet hockey team in the Olympics that year. Their conquest became a defining moment for Brooks and for USA hockey – they seized the opportunity before them in dramatic fashion.

Brooks had no choice but to face the Russians. You, on the other hand, aren't required to act on a point of inflection. But be aware that your defining moment may become a sad tale if you don't act, rather than a legacy that leaves a lasting impact on your business or team. Kodak and Blackberry sat back and look at them now. Don't let inaction define you. Face your challenges and pivot to create the defining moment that you'll look back on with a smile, rather than a shake of your head.

2.   Leading is different than managing

We've established that poor execution is a people problem more than anything else. If you are to be a strong leader during times of change, you must appreciate that leading is different than managing – and that there is a super premium on leadership during times of change.

Winston Churchill is arguably the most famous Briton in history and has gone down in history as its greatest leader. Churchill was very flawed for much of his early career and made huge mistakes in his political life – Gallipoli, the Black and Tans in Ireland, backing use of poison gas. But the entire world's history would have been different if he hadn't come to power in Britain, and led the way that he did, in 1940.[17]

At the moment of truth in May 1940, Churchill was brilliant and inspirational in leading the British people. He knew what had to be done (strategy) and he led through force of will and communication that rallied his country in its 'darkest hour'. Channeling your inner Churchill may be a

---

[17] "Winston Churchill: How a flawed man became a great leader", BBC News, John Simpson, January 23, 2015

bit dramatic but your point of inflection is not the time to rest only on your ability to do things right (good management). It's the time for you to seize the moment to do the right thing (good leadership) and rally your people.

3. Leading requires bold, decisive choices at points of inflection – pick one single over-arching strategy and align with one culture, organization and way of working.

We have a way of complicating things as humans. Good leadership at your point of inflection will be bolstered by keeping it simple – focus on one strategic imperative and ensure that your team is set up for success in pursuing that one mission.

When faced with the specter of Netscape and its internet browsers changing the way that consumers use their personal computing devices, Microsoft was faced with a moment of truth. The decisiveness of Bill Gates' strategy and mission to combat Netscape snuffed out a looming threat to his business and positioned his company as the dominant market application for using the World Wide Web, a way of life for connected consumers around the world.

In the spring of 1993, Marc Andreessen and Eric Bina released Mosaic – the first graphical web browser – when at the National Center for Supercomputing Applications (NCSA). The web browser is the killer app that popularized the internet and became the foundation of the most famous IPO in history at Netscape Communications with a product called "Netscape Navigator." Andreessen and Netscape, founded in early 1994, commercialized the web browser by late 1994 and became household names in 1995 when Netscape went public.

The Netscape IPO in August 1995 became a poster child for the dot-com bubble. By the end of the first day of trading, a 16-month old company with an 8-month old product was valued at nearly $3B – and the company had yet to make a cent of profit. By late 1995, the valuation of the company was nearly three times that first day of trading and its browser commanded an 85% market share.

Over at Microsoft, the dominant personal computing firm had barely embraced the internet, let alone concerned themselves with a company less than two years old. Founded by visionaries, Microsoft had grown so dominant that one might think they didn't need business innovation to succeed but Bill Gates saw the inflection point and acted with swift and decisive action that is rare for a behemoth company.

In an internal memo to his management team in May of 1995, months prior to the successful Netscape IPO, Gates alerted his team to the looming threat in a memo titled "The Internet Tidal Wave." Unsurprisingly, Gates was prescient in his characterization of how the world of computing would evolve. While rich with information on how Microsoft could leverage its strengths to adapt to the internet wave, he was clear in getting their attention.

"One scary possibility being discussed by Internet fans is whether they should get together and create something far less expensive than a PC which is powerful enough for Web browsing." Gates was now aware of Netscape and the power of their browser and its impact on adoption of the internet. His words did not leave room for ambiguity as he noted that "…the internet is a tidal wave. It changes the rules" and proceeded to declare that "now I assign the Internet the highest level of importance." Gates understood what his business needed to do to adapt to this new reality and his words, and actions, were bold and decisive with a singular focus at a critical inflection point for Microsoft.

Microsoft's internet technology investment, and its aggressive business strategy to give away their Internet Explorer browser, led to a dramatic shift in the dominance of internet browsers. By the time that Microsoft introduced v5.0 of Internet Explorer in 1999, Netscape Navigator was all but dead a mere four years removed from its hugely successful IPO. By 2002, Microsoft's Internet Explorer had 90% market share and it was firmly established as the window into the internet for consumers.

Different Flavors of Inflection Points:

Thomson Financial Morphs

Sharon Rowlands was tabbed to lead Thomson Financial (TF) in 1999 at a critical juncture in the company's history as it found itself "stuck in the middle" between upstart internet companies and the 800-pound gorillas of the financial information industry, Bloomberg and Reuters. TF experienced two decades of explosive growth as a fiercely decentralized portfolio of financial information companies that provided online data to all segments of the financial community and grew to $2B in revenues by the late 1990s. By then, the world of financial information started to change rapidly.

The internet boom of the 1990s saw the introduction of upstart competition that liberated content and delivered lower quality – yet significantly lower priced – information to the industry and TF's massively profitable businesses struggled to defend its customer base – and margins – in this new era. Unfortunately, TF was limited in its options to compete if it maintained its decentralized heritage.

To its credit, the Thomson Corporation saw it coming. But it wasn't easy to make dramatic changes to a portfolio of businesses that had such strong historical growth and massive EBITDA margins. In fact, there was no drive to change from *within* the business because these decentralized businesses were led by CEOs that liked being masters of their domains *and* those CEOs were compensated in line with margin growth so they did not embrace the need for a different view of the long game if it impacted their near-term compensation. To make matters worse, short-term margin growth was much easier to achieve by price increases to dominant information sources, rather than by investing in product innovation that created entry barriers for competition. TF was being set up for a major comeuppance.

The meeting called by the aforementioned client at Bankers Trust was an inadvertent flash mob that signaled the clear need for a turning point in the strategy at TF. Sharon's instincts knew that a change was needed but the burning platform for change was lit by the client at Bankers Trust who made it obvious that it was unacceptable for 25 sales reps to be selling independent products rather than simplifying the relationship *and* creating more value for the client. For Sharon, the point of inflection was clear: TF needed to organize around client solutions that combined its assets to defend themselves against the upstart point solutions, solve higher-end problems for the client, and create a large expense rationalization by combining 25 separate businesses into one operating company organized around client solutions. Besides, the clients were starting to *insist!* Sounds easy, right?

Fast forward two years, powered by the Thomson ONE platform, TF wins the largest contract in financial information industry history to provide the wealth management work stations for Merrill Lynch in 2002. The headlines in major newspapers created a remarkable validation for the transformation of the business to compete with the likes of Reuters and Bloomberg. The transformation evolved over four years after these headlines and to say that the transformation was hard may be an understatement to Rowlands. After five years, three of the original 40 senior executives from 2000 remained with TF as the metamorphosis from decentralized businesses led to massive casualties. Strong people – yet with the wrong team orientation for the new strategy – had to be moved out. Change can be hard, but necessary.

Looking back on this massive inflection point, Rowlands is quick to point out that "the most important thing is that the team is aligned." Strategic decisions are important but strategic *actions* are the key to success and people are the drivers of those actions.

GAIN Capital Busts Out of Its Straight Jacket

Online trading of stocks started in the mid-1980s via services on AOL and CompuServ. By the late 1990s, internet-based stock trading for retail investors was becoming commonplace via services like eTrade.com. For those retail investors interested in trading foreign exchange, though, access to currency markets was limited and expensive at that time. Not until Forex.com launched trading via streaming rates on the internet in 2004 was the U.S. investor able to trade currencies online in this way. Forex.com was first mover in the U.S. allowing online traders to 'click-and-deal' from streaming rates for currencies, rather than the traditional method of requesting quotes in a very non-real-time, and expensive, manner.

Forex.com had about a one-year head start in the U.S. market trading currencies in this manner. Growth was dramatic for this young company as the new market expanded and competitors were scarce. By 2010, though, market growth had slowed in the U.S. and competitors were becoming numerous. To maintain a strong growth profile, a moment of truth slowly crept up on Forex's parent company GAIN Capital - the high growth associated with early entrants in a new market stalled and it was clear that GAIN's revenue growth would have to come from global trading markets beyond the U.S. That said, global markets were more sophisticated than U.S. markets for retail derivatives trading and GAIN would have to evolve to support trading a much broader range of instruments that were more complex than simple currency pairs – so complex that the proprietary GAIN platform did not properly support these new instruments.

GAIN's challenge at this moment of truth was to find the best way to support trading of a global range of instruments to grow its business but it was saddled with a trading platform that wasn't prepared to do that. Buy v. Build decisions occur all the time for businesses and this particular buy v. build decision had big strategic implications for GAIN. It would take years, if not more, to get the existing platform to support the global range of products yet it would take a very large financial investment to buy competitors. Timing was important and, as GAIN's CEO put it, "...you can't let your organic growth ego get in the way."

Under CEO Glenn Stevens' leadership, GAIN charged into its inflection point with bold ambition, as well as a hedge to support an organic fallback plan (as any good trader would create). GAIN placed minor bets on building to extend the existing platform but soon started on a path of serial acquisitions that would give it command of the market in the U.S. and establish an important foothold in Europe to lay the foundation for global trading. Over the course of three years starting in 2012, Stevens closed and integrated six acquisitions to bolster GAIN's U.S. and Global businesses.

Resting on its laurels would have made for a lot less work but GAIN chose the bold path and rolled up the industry in the U.S. The growth of GAIN's revenues and client accounts continued to roll through the 10s under Stevens' leadership.

Accuity Awakens A Sleeping Giant (Itself)

There aren't many businesses in the U.S. that have been in existence since 1836. There are even fewer that have been around for that period of time without significantly changing their business model but that's exactly what characterized Thomson Financial Publishing (TFP) in 2006. TFP published bank directories that were omnipresent in banks through the 20th century to help their operations properly process checks and payments in a world where routing numbers were not digitally available. As the official registrar of American Banking Association (ABA) routing numbers since 1911, TFP had command of a small niche in the market for routing number information in the U.S.

After a decade of no growth up to 2004, the business was sold to new private equity owners as part of a larger media portfolio. The new owners wanted to either break out of the no growth rut or divest the TFP business and focus on the other media assets. In light of limited U.S. banking growth, and a general decline in the print medium, TFP had been strong and steady but did not show the signs of life that a new owner often desires. TFP's leaders had to create an inflection point for this business or this 180-year old business was at risk of being sold to new owners or, worse, managed for short-term returns and not long-term viability.

New president, Hugh Jones, had a challenging task but was also aware of the unique data assets in the business that were stuck in a product and revenue model with a dependency on print and on traditional customer perceptions of TFP. Creating inflection points for a business can often happen around a singular change in strategy yet, in this case, a wave of changes were needed to break out of a 180-year rhythm.

The goal was to change the conversation with customers about the solutions and *value* delivered by this venerable old business. Expanding digital solutions from its wealth of banking data was a surmountable challenge within Jones' grasp yet changing perceptions of TFP was tricky. Starting with a rebrand of the legacy TFP brand to Accuity, the company began to enlighten customers of the powerful value add to their operations when Accuity data solutions were utilized to streamline payments and save money.

Instead of selling by using the traditional price book for Accuity data, Jones made a simple, yet powerful, rule for his sales team. Jones' rule was that "we do not discuss price until we've established value with the client." Understanding banking client needs *first* led to an enlightenment of the true value of Accuity data solutions in the eyes the client. Value-based pricing exercises led to more revenue for Accuity but also a very clear and significant realization of the value proposition for the client.

Accuity captured value while clients looked like stars when they could fully articulate savings within their operation. Jones and his team presented a crisp value story in terms of dollars and cents and the tide started to turn…and this turning point came in 2008-09 when the banking industry was experiencing its toughest financial stretch in many decades!

Once established as a data solutions provider, Accuity began to grow its global footprint and its product lines to find a very strong growth curve for its owners. (You might say that Accuity had the longest top to their S-curve in U.S. business history before Jones arrived!). By the time of its sale in 2011, Accuity had gone from being the tired print asset that was on the cusp of a quick sale to the crown jewel of the portfolio. Creating inflection points is hard work but, done right, can provide dramatic returns for its investors and leaders.

Tough Decisions

Inflection points are inevitable but the decision to act is not trivial. Charging off half-cocked to conquer your business challenge is not advised. Ensure that you've thoughtfully considered your alternative strategies, your organization's ability to execute, your opportunity costs with a new strategy, and whether your most important stakeholders will buy into your new direction.

The wholesale strategy change by Thomson Financial was bold. Frankly, executive management had little idea of the massive heavy lifting required to execute strategy, organization, and operational changes all at once…in sync. The new strategy worked in the end but what if there were missteps, or indecision, that delayed the metamorphosis by years, or forever? While your business is making big changes, some of your competition will be making tactical changes to creep ahead and you may lose ground to them while you are getting traction with your new direction. The time in transition matters so make sure you go 'all in'. The faster you move, the less time there is for competitors to capitalize on your transition.

The M&A strategy at GAIN Capital was aggressive. As we know, nearly 70% of acquisitions fail to live up to their investment cases due to a lack of execution so the GAIN strategy to extract cost synergies from similar businesses had to be executed with precision. But what if they weren't precise? Cost synergies are good but would GAIN have been better served using a percentage of that capital investment to grow products and sales organically? Would collateral damage to human capital have been eliminated with an organic strategy v. the acquisition route? GAIN gracefully managed their aggressive acquisition plan but you must ensure that you are prepared to execute with great care or your opportunity costs may become painfully material.

The repositioning of the Accuity business toward digital solutions with value-based selling was a confident, yet hopeful, endeavor. While the leverage of data into higher-end solutions made perfect sense to the leaders of this business, would key stakeholders believe you when you change the conversation about a business that has been doing the same thing for so many years? In the case of Accuity, clients saw them as a 175-year old business that printed bank directories, would they struggle to see them suddenly as a digital company adding higher-order value? Would employees struggle to get behind the business repositioning and slow their ambition to change? In their case, Accuity really had no choice and were mindful of all the minds they had to change.

At the end of the day, leaders have to make tough decisions often. When making changes that impact many, there will be times where you are questioned – even criticized – and there may even be times when you question yourself. Be brave and stick to your leadership values and commitment to the end game. Your faith in doing the right thing for the business will super cede doubters in the long run when you have the right team tightly aligned to ride along with you on your changes.

A New Strategic Direction Is Upon You – What Do You Do?

Some of you will be the catalysts of change that recognize the need for a point of inflection and set a new direction. Many of you, though, will be leaders that are inheriting a new strategic direction from executive management. It has been thrust upon you, often with you having little input, and you are a key leader in executing on this change that you've just inherited. It may make perfect sense and you may be completely energized to charge the hill to execute on the new vision. Or it may not. But, *it doesn't matter.*

It doesn't matter if you think there are flaws in the new direction. It doesn't matter if you weren't intimately involved in the new direction. It doesn't matter if you think it will make life more difficult for you and your peers. What matters is that many strategies are viable yet *all* strategies rely upon a team of leaders that are bought in and aligned to make it happen. If you aren't going to be one of those aligned leaders, you might consider your options sooner than later.

If you don't want to be one of those (former) leaders that got run over by change, here are some ground rules to ensure that you are at the leading edge of change in your company:

1. Embrace change

Don't be that person that executive management has to question whether you're on the bus. (Because you'll be under the bus if you don't). Instead of being a suspect, you may instead be that leader that executive management pushes to the front of the class because they see you as the type of leader needed to navigate change. Going back to our Thomson Financial story, Sharon Rowlands was working three levels below the CEO of the Thomson Corporation – and an ocean away from its U.S. headquarters – when she was identified as the right type of leader to carry TF forward in a brave new era. Her actions, and her words, filled management with confidence that she would say, and do, the right things to lead TF.

2. Don't show any signs of resistance

If you believe there are flaws in the new direction, there is a right way and a wrong way to make your point. First and foremost, your first move should not be to highlight flaws over opportunities. Although your observations may be correct, it's not what the executive management catalyzing changes wants to hear first. People that are viewed as "glass half empty" in the very early days will be people that get pushed to the side.

3. Digest the strategic goals and translate them to your organization's mission

Waste no time in understanding the new strategic goals and crafting the role of your organization in this change. It is imperative that you help your team understand and that you create a clear line of sight between their mission and actions and the grand vision. Like yourself, you want to help your team be the embracers of change, not the resistance.

4. In public and private, get behind the strategy – and maybe even evangelize

There is a fine line between rhetoric about the strategic change and authentic communication about the change. Be sincere. Be a good listener and address the questions and fears that people have with a sense of ownership for the new direction. Most importantly, what you say in private is just as important as what you say in public because your sincerity will evaporate quickly in the face of one private conversation that gets divulged against your wishes.

It's okay to be realistic about the challenges of change but always do so with a glass half full. Every communication matters.

The turning point for your business, and your team, is here. It's time to put your leadership on display and have a professional experience that you'll be proud of. It's time for your BRAVE leadership...you can do it.

1 *Environment*: Clarify Your Situation and Field of Play

Leaders often react to their new situations by asking, "What have I gotten myself into?" That is exactly the right question. As Steven Covey put it, "Seek first to understand." Seek to understand the context for your leadership and then make choices around where to focus with that context in mind. This will make things in the future much more straightforward.

For the late Zappos CEO Tony Hsieh, the most important decision is where to play. He learned that playing poker. He applied it at Zappos. In Hsieh's words:

> *"Through reading poker books and practicing by playing, I spent a lot of time learning about the best strategy to play once I was actually sitting down at a table. My big 'ah-ha!' moment came when I finally learned that the game started even before I sat down in a seat.*
>
> *In a poker room at a casino, there are usually many different choices of tables. Each table has different stakes, different players, and different dynamics that change as the players come and go, and as players get excited, upset, or tired.*
>
> *I learned that the most important decision I could make was which table to sit at."*[18]

We suggest thinking about this in three steps: What? So what? Now what?[19]

1. Understand the organization's history, recent results and potential scenarios for business and competitive conditions. (What.)
2. Align around an interpretation of the situation assessment (So what.)
3. Make choices around where to play and where not to play (Now what.)

---

[18] from "Delivering Happiness", Tony Hsieh
[19] For more on this framework see George Bradt's December 5, 2012 Forbes.com: article "Three Essential Questions of Big Data: What? So What? Now What?"

1. Understand Context

The context for your leadership is made up of the organization's history, recent results and scenarios for business and competitive conditions.

Organizational History

If you see a static picture of a pencil on a table you can only guess in which direction the pencil is rolling. If you see part of a video of a pencil rolling across a table, the direction of its roll is readily apparent. The same is true with an organization. Knowing how it started and developed are valuable inputs into understanding its direction.

Hewlett Packard began in a garage. It developed as a family company, seeped in the founder's values and "way." A couple of recent CEOs of Hewlett Packard ignored that history and tried to move the organization forward in ways that did not work. Don't do that. Understand the history.

Yearley/Toll Example[20]

Put yourself in Doug Yearley's shoes in November 2009. You've just been named EVP on the way to becoming CEO of luxury homebuilder Toll Brothers, a company that lost $750 million in the year that just ended due to accounting write-downs. You're entering the fifth year of a recession in your industry. Your core revenues were down 44 percent versus the prior year, and 75 percent versus the peak a few years before. If there was ever an organization that required significant change, this was it. Right?

Wrong. Yearley had to engage this culture and his colleagues in the right context. Doug knew three things as he transitioned into his role as the second CEO ever at the company:

1. The organization was strong. It had cash in the bank and solid processes in place, including a long-standing management review every Monday evening.

---

[20] From George Bradt's October 5, 2011 Forbes.com article, "Despite Bleak Housing Market, Toll Brothers CEO Isn't Panicking"

2. He was an integral part of that organization. Yearley had been there for 20 years and steadily progressed as a leader. At the point he took over from Robert Toll as CEO in June 2010, he had spent 800 Monday evenings with Robert on those management calls.

3. He knew what he could control, and what he could not control, and he was confident that Toll would come through the dark days and emerge stronger.

Two years later, it looked like they were weathering the storm. Even though the housing market was still bleak, Toll had just announced its fifth straight quarterly profits. As Yearley was quick to point out, not enough profits – but they were profits. They had $4.2 billion cash and $800 million in available credit.

Yearley, Robert Toll and their team did a couple of things right in line with the Stockdale paradox.[21]

Face the Brutal Truths Head On

First, they faced the brutal truths head on. As Yearley explained to George *"This incredibly deep and dark housing recession is like none we've ever seen before."* They were continually "right sizing" where they had to, centralizing purchasing and watching incentives. They were managing cash carefully. Delivering even small profits with revenues down 75 percent is no mean trick.

Position for Future Success

Second, they were positioning themselves to take advantage of the upturn when it comes. As Yearley told George,

---

[21] As described by Jim Collins in "Good to Great" in thinking about how Admiral James Stockdale led his fellow prisoners in the Vietnam War: "You must retain faith that you will prevail in the end, regardless of the difficulties. AND at the same time…You must confront the most brutal facts of your current reality, whatever they might be."

Because we have a strong cash position and balance sheet…I can challenge the company to look into new ideas…This keeps it exciting for people even though sales may not be where we want them to be.

Those new ideas included:

- Continuing their push into urban (started in 2003 – 22 percent of their revenues now come from high-rises in New York)
- Looking at international opportunities
- Establishing Gibraltar Capital to buy distressed portfolios of loans
- Looking at new markets within the United States

What Yearley did not do was panic. He did not shock the system. He was confident that he and his team could continue to right size the company, grow and return to meaningful profitability.

Implications for you: Understand the context. It may change your mind about what to do.

Understand as much as you can about the spark that created the organization, the founders, and the early "starter" team, how it developed, its stories and myths. They are all real – in at least some members' minds. Do this on a macro level for the entire organization, getting at its fundamental nature – design, produce, deliver, service. Do this on a micro level for whatever team you are called to lead, understanding its role and contribution. Do this on a personal level for the most important individual members of the team so you understand their individual stories.

Recent Results

The second piece of context is recent results. Surprise surprise - an organization that has been performing well and meeting its goals is going to be less open to change than one that has been missing targets. The level of confidence of team members used to winning will be different than the level of those who have had setbacks.

Similar to history, look at recent results on organizational, team, and individual levels.

Business Environment: 5Cs Situation Assessment

As a leader, you'll find it helpful to have some frameworks for your thinking. (And we did promise we'd give you frameworks and tools.) The 5Cs Situation Assessment is a framework for understanding the business environment by looking at customers, collaborators, capabilities, competitors, and conditions:

> **Customers**: First line, customer chain, end users, influencers.
> **Collaborators**: Suppliers, allies, government/community leaders.
> **Capabilities**: Human, operational, financial, technical, key assets.
> **Competitors**: Direct, indirect, potential.
> **Conditions**: Social/demographic/health, political/government/ regulatory, economic, technical, market, climate.

Think 1) **What**: Objective, scientific truths – facts. 2) **So what**: Subjective, personal, cultural or political truths, opinions, assumptions, judgments, conclusions. 3) **Now what**: Indicated actions.

Customers

Customers include the people your organization sells to or serves. These comprise direct customers who actually give you money, as well as their customers, their customers' customers, and so on down the line. Eventually, there are end users or consumers of whatever the output of that chain is. Additionally, there are the people who influence your various customers' purchase decisions. Take all of these into account.

Federal Express sells overnight delivery services to corporate purchasing departments that contract those services on behalf of business managers. But the real decision makers have historically been those managers' administrative assistants. So, Federal Express targeted its marketing efforts not at the people who write the checks, not at the managers, but at the core influencers. They aimed advertising and media at those influencers and had their drivers pick the packages up from the administrative assistants personally instead of going through an impersonal mailroom.

Collaborators

Collaborators include your suppliers, business allies, and people delivering complementary products and services across your eco-system. What links all these groups together is that they will do better if you do better. So, it's in their best interest, whether they know it or not, to help you succeed. Think Microsoft and Intel. Think hot dogs and mustard.

Just as these relationships are two-way, so must be your analysis. You need to understand the interdependencies and reciprocal commitments. Whenever these dependencies and commitments are out of balance, the nature of the relationships will inevitably change.

Think through your customer's purchasing cycle. Who comes before you? Who comes after you? If you're in corporate real estate, a relocation expert you can vouch for and trust is an obvious ally. However, a printing business could be your ally as your customer will need new letterhead and business cards to reflect their new location.

Collaborators are strategic partnerships, so think strategically. The less resources you control in-house, the more important this is.

Capabilities

Capabilities are those abilities that can help you deliver a differentiated, better product or service to your customers. These abilities include everything from access to materials and capital to plants and equipment to people to patents. Pay particular attention to people, plans, and practices.

Competitors

Competitors are those to whom your customers could give their money or attention instead of to you. It is important to take a wide view of potential competitors. Amtrak's real competitors are other forms of transportation like automobiles and airplanes. The competition for consumer dollars may be as varied as a child's college education versus a Disney World vacation. In analyzing these competitors, it is important to think through their objectives, strategies and situation, as well as strengths and weaknesses to better understand and predict what they might do next and over time.

Conditions

Conditions are a catchall for everything going on in the environment in which you do business. At the least, look at socio/demographic, political, economic, technology and climate trends and determine how they might impact the organization over the short-, mid-, and long term.

Macro elements:
- Social/demographic/health
- Political/government/regulatory
- Economic
- Technology
- Market – including consolidations and cross-vertical expansion
- Climate/weather.

5Cs Situation analysis Guidelines

1. Customers (First line, customer chain, end users, influencers)
Needs, hopes, preferences, commitments, strategies, price/value perspectives by segment.

First line/direct customers
- Universe of opportunity—total market, volume by segment.
- Current situation—volume by customer; profit by customer.

Customer chain
- Customers' customers—total market, volume by segment.
- Current customers' strategies, volume and profitability by segment.

End users
- Preference, consumption, usage, loyalty, and price value data and perceptions for our products and competitors' products.

Influencers
- Key influencers of customer and end user purchase and usage decisions.

2. Collaborators (Suppliers, allies, partners, government/community leaders in eco-system)
- Strategies, profit/value models for external and internal stakeholders (up, across, down).

3. Capabilities

Human (includes style and quality of management, strategy dissemination, culture)

Operational (includes integrity of business processes, effectiveness of organization structure, links between measures and rewards, and corporate governance)

Financial (includes capital and asset utilization and investor management)

Technical (includes core processes, IT systems, supporting skills)

Key assets (includes brands and intellectual property)

4. Competitors (Direct, indirect, potential).
- Strategies, profit/value models, profit pools by segment, source of pride.

5. Conditions
- Social/demographic/health—trends
- Political/government/regulatory—trends
- Economic—macro and micro—trends
- Technical – trends and disruptions
- Market definition, inflows, outflows, substitutes —trends including consolidation and cross-vertical expansion
- Climate change impact on your organization

Pulling it together: SWOT analysis and thinking about:
- Sources, drivers, hinderers of revenue, profits, and value.
- Current strategy/resource deployment: Coherent? Adequate? Defacto strategy?
- Insights and scenarios (To set up: What/So what/Now what?)

2. Align around an Interpretation of the Situation Assessment

Leadership is about inspiring, enabling and empowering others. Understanding the context for your leadership is necessary at a point of inflection, but not sufficient. You're not done until your team is aligned around an interpretation of that context. Of course, individual team members will have their own different perspectives. This is not about getting to 100 percent congruence. It is about getting to a consensus around the most important elements, how people feel about them – "So what?"

SWOT

A SWOT (internal Strengths and Weaknesses versus external Opportunities and Threats) analysis drives consensus key leverage points, business issues, and sustainable competitive advantages.

Look at this in the context of your mission, vision, nature of your business.

Strengths: internal resources and capabilities yielding advantages.

Weaknesses: internal resource and capability gaps yielding vulnerabilities.

Opportunities: things happening in the world outside the organization that should make it easier for the organization to succeed. People often get this wrong, putting in ideas here around what the organization might do. Don't do that yet. Follow the process and keep this section focused on things happening outside the organization.

Threats: things happening in the world outside the organization that make it more difficult for the organization to sustain or succeed. Remember to keep this focused on external threats.

Key leverage points: internal strengths that can be brought to bear to take advantage of external opportunities. These are the corridors of ways to win through your point of inflection. For example, if you have a strong beverage distribution system and the public water supply is contaminated, you could leverage your system to deliver safe bottled water to people. This is the first of the "So what?" thinking sections.

Business issues: areas of internal weakness that are particularly vulnerable to external threats. Fixing these is a way to avoid losing. If you have only marginally acceptable safety standards in your plants and there is pending legislation to increase legal safety standards well beyond those that you currently meet, that is a potential issue. This is the second of the "So what?" thinking sections.

Finally, the *sustainable competitive advantage* is most likely one of the key leverage points that can be sustained in the face of business issues.

You'll find yourself using SWOTs over and over again. Gillian has often used it as a team exercise, as it gets everyone on board aligned with vision and strategy and starting to think in terms of "So what?"

Biases - Make sure you're correcting for potential biases including:[22]

Negative bias: When you have a negative experience, it has a larger impact on your memory and leads you to believe that certain roads are to be avoided, to a greater degree, than a quantitative analysis would demonstrate.

Frequency bias: When you hear or see something repeatedly over time, you will be more inclined to believe it.

Recent Bias: When making a decision, something you learned just recently will often carry more weight than information you learned a while ago.

Attachment bias: Leaders can very easily become overly conservative and avoid making the right decision, simply because they don't want to disrupt the status quo, which they helped achieve.

Escalation bias: When you start down a path, you look for evidence to support your direction and at your peril, choose to ignore warning signs.

---

[22] From Gary R. Cohen's Ivy Business Journal July/August 2020 article on Just Ask Leadership: Why Great Managers Always Ask the Right Questions.

SWOT

View in context of mission, vision, & nature of business (develop, produce, deliver, service)

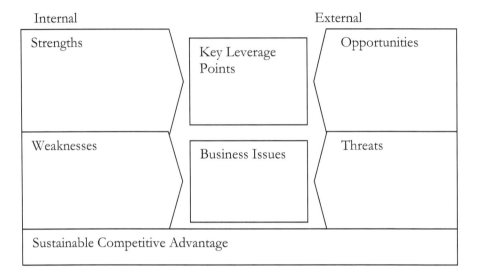

Strengths   Internal to organization - things we do better
Weaknesses   Internal to organization - things we do worse
Opportunities External to organization - things to capitalize on
Threats   External to organization - things to worry about

Key Leverage Points: Opportunities against which we can leverage our strengths (where play to win)

Business Implications: Threats to which our weaknesses make us vulnerable (where to play not to lose)

Sustainable Competitive Advantages - Key leverage points that can be sustained over extended period of time.

Another valuable tool gets at where value is created – Gadiesh and Gilber's Profit Pools Tool. On the one hand, it's deceptively simple. Map revenue on the horizontal axis and operating margin on the vertical axis. Out pops a graphic showing you the relative size of the profit pools. On the other hand, it tends to reveal some surprising things. For example, in the 1980s, a surprisingly large portion of the auto industry's profits was in car financing.

TOOL 1.3
PROFIT POOLS

Operating Margin
100%
90%
80%
70%
60%
50%
40%
30%
20%
10%
0%

| 0% | Share of industry revenue | 100% |

Per Orit Gadiesh and James Gilber, "A Fresh Look at Strategy" *Harvard Business Review,* May 1998

To customize this document, download Tool 1.3 from the BRAVE Leadership page on www.onboardingtools.com.

Complete the SWOT analysis.

Use it (and profit pools where appropriate) to help you understand the sources, drivers, hinderers of revenue, and value.

Take a look at the current strategy/resource deployment: Coherent? Adequate? Defacto strategy?

Think through your insights and potential scenarios (To complete "So what" and set up "Now what?" choices.)

3. Make choices around where to play and where not to play

With the first two parts complete, you're now ready to make your choices around where to play and where not to play.

We keep learning the same lesson over and over again – or not.[23] Porter told us that strategy is choosing what not to do. Choosing not to focus is choosing to be average at everything. And average does not win.

Marakon's[24] Neal Kissel sent me their latest research showing yet again that "the path to superior performance is determined by management's decisions about where to focus the firm's strategic resources (time, people and capital)."

They looked at 1,200 companies and found that "60-75% of the variation in performance between companies in **the same sector** can be explained by high level choices about where resources should be focused."

You'd think everyone would understand this by now. Study authors Kissel, Formstone, Foley and Ramos point out five reasons why more CEOs don't act on it:

1. **"It's outside of the comfort zone of senior managers** whose typical path to top roles is via a track record of delivering sustained operational improvement, rather than through making better portfolio choices;

2. Continuing with the **status quo feels less risky** than taking bold decisions on future strategic focus and portfolio shape;

3. Successful strategic resource management requires hard choices about whose business to starve, or exit, in order to invest behind others, but **CEOs don't like saying no** to the executives running those businesses and this often results in 'peanut butter' spreading;

4. The **annual budgeting and planning games get in the way,** as the battle to win extra resources crowds out decisions on future shape and investment priorities; and

5. **Nobody likes missing budget,** so the pressure to deliver quarterly earnings means that when push comes to shove harder strategic choices get deferred."

---

[23] Adapted from George Bradt's October 15, 2019 Forbes.com article, "Why Where To Play Must Be Your First Choice"
[24] Marakon Strategic Advisory is part of Charles Rivers Associates

With these in mind, they then go on to suggest six ways for CEOs to deal with this:

1. **"Understand their starting point:** Build a granular view on the value created for the company and customers in the existing portfolio (e.g., by geography, sub-sector, product segment, customer).

2. **Develop a view of the trend line:** Look at how customer needs and behaviours are changing and the implications for where value will be created in the future.

3. **Put in place a disciplined financial framework:** Set high standards for reinvestment in the business, optimize balance sheet leverage, and be willing to raise external finance to pursue value creating opportunities.

4. **Optimise the use of all resources:** Adopt a zero-based approach to resource allocation, use the annual processes to look at 100% of the capital and talent base. Concentrate resources on businesses where they can sustain or build valuable differences and continuously ask whether there is a higher value use for any of the resources they control.

5. **Actively reshape their portfolio:** Use acquisitions and divestiture to accelerate the reallocation of capital and other resources to the highest value opportunities, with a strong internal finance and M&A capability to support a continuous programmatic approach.

6. **Invest behind intangibles**: Ensure they are customer focused, innovate to remain on trend and build reputational and brand value to sustain profitable growth in the long-term."

The difference between where to play and how to win

1. It's not an either/or choice. You have to get both right. Strategy is about the creation and allocation of resources to the right place in the right way at the right time over time. Question #1, where to play goes to the right place. You must make the "high level choices about where resources should be focused." This is the art of the general.

2. Then get aligned on what matters and why and work with your captains to figure out the "right way", how to win. That's how you deliver consistent over-performance.

Play to your strengths. We've learned this over and over again. It's far more productive to build on your strengths than to correct your weaknesses. Mathematically, adding 10 percent where you have a large market share is always more valuable than adding 10 percent where you have a small share.

Chalef/Knowledge Tree Example

Where to play is generally the first of the five core questions a BRAVE leader needs to answer. In theory, you should choose which customers to serve and which of their problem to solve. Industries and competitors, business models, places in the value chain, and geography should all play a role in your choices.

But as infamous computer scientist Jan L. A. van de Snepscheut noted, *"In theory, there is no difference between theory and practice. But in practice, there is."* Just ask KnowledgeTree's CEO Daniel Chalef.

Which Problem to Solve

Founded as a systems integrator, KnowledgeTree soon understood its customers needed document management. So Chalef and his team built an open source document manager, which worked so well that increasingly more people found it and used it over time. Soon, KnowledgeTree's core business morphed. As Chalef told George, *"The market found us as opposed to us looking for a problem to solve."*

Which Business Model

KnowledgeTree's business model continues to evolve. Having moved into the document management business, it realized the future was in the cloud and changed from helping people manage documents behind the firewall to helping them manage documents in the cloud. Then it realized that just managing documents wasn't enough, and built tools and skills to curate, use, and draw insights from documents to solve *"higher order problems."*

Value Chain Focal Point

Similarly, KnowledgeTree's value chain focus has changed. Chalef suggests all start-ups need to be ready to change. *"In a start up, it's dynamic."* In KnowledgeTree's case, it began with design and is now focused on delivery. Chalef suspects they'll need to build out more and more support capabilities as they work with ever-larger customers.

Geography

For many, there's a geographical dimension to the where to play question. Michael Porter et al have made a strong case for the power of geographically clustered industry hubs like film in Hollywood and Bollywood and fashion design in Milan.

Chalef started KnowledgeTree in South Africa. As it expanded, he looked for the optimal place to locate his business. He was initially attracted to Silicon Valley but quickly realized the time-zone difference with South Africa was too challenging, so he contemplated Boston. Unfortunately, the South African-native wasn't in favor of winter weather. Enter Raleigh, North Carolina, which offered a technology cluster in a time zone closer to his South African developers and a more moderate climate.

Where to play in Practice

Where to play choices:
- Which problem to solve (for which customers?)
- Which business model?
- Value chain focal point?
- Geography?

Don't get us wrong. Having a framework is important. Customers and their problems, your business model, value chain, and geographic choices are important. Just don't follow the theory off the cliff. Theoretically elegant has no value if it's not practically useful. Chalef says he made his decisions partly with scientific methods and partly with gut feel. Not a bad way to approach getting the best of theory and practice.[25]

Implications for you: Take into account the theoretical, but drive to the practical.

Nike used an interesting approach in its expansion, changing only one variable at a time through points of inflection. For example, their first entry into any international market was with running shoes branded Nike.

	Sport	Item	Brand	Geography
Base:	Running	Shoes	Nike	USA
New sport:	**GOLF**	Shoes	Nike	USA
New item:	Running	**HATS**	Nike	USA
New brand:	Running	Shoes	**AIR JORDAN**	USA
New geography:	Running	Shoes	Nike	**JAPAN**

---

[25] From George Bradt's November 21, 2012 Forbes.com article, "Where Should You Play: When Theory and Practice Diverge"

Ideally, you can find ways to leverage your strengths against new and emerging opportunities. Ideally, you can find ways to do this requiring you to change as few variables as possible.

Of course, you have to do some work to shore up your areas of vulnerability. If your boat has a hole in it below the water line, fix it. But fixing the hole won't win you the race. It will just keep you from losing.

Patrick/Proxima and Carticept Example[26]

"Where it matters and where you can win" is the answer to the first of the five most important questions for BRAVE leaders, "Where to play?"

George's wife and he had a mantra when their children were little. They only confronted the kids when a) it mattered and b) they could win. What mattered tended to be things making material differences to the children's well-being or putting themselves or others at risk. Generally, they could win things that did not violate basic laws of nature. (For example, trying to get a two-week-old to sleep through the night was a non-starter.)

This framework works for organizations as well. Choose to play where it matters and where you can win.

Look at this from several different levels, taking into account the macro environment, your organization's place in the macro environment, and your place in your organization. Across those levels, what matters are generally things aligned with meaningful and rewarding shared purposes. Where you can win generally involves some sort of sustainable competitive advantage that doesn't defy the laws of nature.

Tim Patrick has done this twice: at Proxima and at Carticept.

---

[26] From George Bradt's November 7, 2012 Forbes.com article, "Where Should You Play? The Secret to Investing Your Time and Talent for Maximum Impact and Reward"

Proxima

When researchers at Johns Hopkins developed a unique way of radiating cancer allowing quicker and more efficient treatment, Patrick saw this as a partnership opportunity. Together, they used this technology on brain cancers with positive results. Patrick also realized he could take that technology and apply it to other cancers. While there were 20,000 incidents of brain cancer in the United States, there were 200,000 incidents of breast cancer. So, Patrick built Proxima to play in that space, solving an unmet clinical need, making a positive impact on patients, and generating a good financial return. It mattered. They could win.

Carticept

Having sold Proxima, Patrick next looked at the aging population and the more than 40 million people in the United States who suffer or will suffer from some form of arthritis. Many of them will need joint replacements. That matters to a lot of people. But Patrick realized he couldn't win there. Why? The big orthopedic companies were well established in the space.

The unmet clinical need was in the area of steroid injections. Other than the publicity surrounding some sports heroes (and fallen heroes,) this area was getting relatively little attention. Enter Carticept's portable ultrasound-guided injections, dramatically improving the accuracy of local applications of steroids to local injuries. Once again, Patrick had identified an unmet clinical need that mattered and where his organization could win.

But the world has changed. It's tougher and takes longer to get FDA (Food and Drug Administration) approvals than it did when Patrick was building Proxima. At Proxima, Patrick sprinted. He created a culture of risk takers to build the business fast and sell it. At Carticept, Patrick is running a marathon. So he's built a different culture and formed a strategic partnership with SonoSite to cross-distribute products and generate revenues to fund the extra time he needs to get his approvals. He's playing where it matters and where he can win, just differently.

Where it matters and where you can win

Where it matters is most likely going to be where there is an unmet need that has a meaningful impact on peoples' lives. Where you can win is not just where you have strengths, but where you have differentiated strengths from others playing around your space.[27]

Implications for you: There is no value in sameness. Be different.

The "Now what?" of where to play is to take the "So what?" consensus alignment around your "What?" context and make choices around where to play – and not play.

George once asked one of his bosses to help prioritize ten tasks he was working on. His boss said they were all "A" priority. George replied that that meant they were all the same and therefore "A" meant average. For something to be top priority, something else must be lower priority.

Remember that when delegating tasks to your team.

Choosing where to play is necessary, but not sufficient. You must also choose where not to play. Choose to

- **Maintain or divest** less attractive areas where you have a competitive advantage
- **Invest** in more attractive areas where you have a competitive advantage
- Perhaps **build** advantages in more attractive areas where you do not have a competitive advantage – if the return-on -nvestment works
- **Avoid** less attractive areas where you do not have a competitive advantage

---

[27] From George Bradt's November 7, 2012 Forbes.com article, "Where Should You Play? The Secret to Investing Your Time and Talent for Maximum Impact and Reward"

TOOL 1.4
WHERE TO PLAY CHOICES

Areas where we have Competitive advantages	Maintain? Divest?		Invest
Areas where we do not have Competitive advantages	Not now Not ever		Build for later?
	Less attractive areas		More attractive areas

Summary: Where to Play

One of the most important choices you and your team make is where to play. You must understand the context in which you're operating and interpret and create context for others as you lead through a point of inflection. Today's environment is highly charged in exciting and dangerous ways. So be sure to consider all the risks and opportunities both outside and inside your field of endeavor and organization.

- Understand the organization's history, recent results, and changes and scenarios for business and competitive conditions.
- Align around an interpretation of the situation assessment.
- Make choices around where to play and where not to play within your context.
- Don't try to be everything to everyone. **

2 *Values*: Align All Around the Organization's Mission, Vision, and Guiding Principles

Leadership is about inspiring, enabling and empowering others to do their absolute best together to realize a meaningful and rewarding shared purpose. What matters is that shared purpose.

Virtually every experienced leader that spoke at CEO Connection CEO Boot Camps through the years has said that the number one job of any leader is to own the vision and values. It's true for experienced CEOs. It's true for first-time leaders. It's true for everyone in between. Get clear on your purpose – your mission, vision, and guiding principles.

Simon Sinek put it particularly well in his September 2009 TED talk in which he explained his "golden circle" of communicating from the "why" out instead of the "what" in.

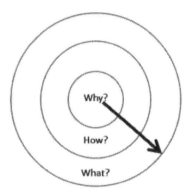

Why? How? What? This little idea explains why some organizations and some leaders are able to inspire where others aren't...

And by "why" I don't mean "to make a profit." That's a result.

By "why" I mean: what's your purpose? What's your cause? What's your belief? Why does your organization exist? Why do you get out of bed in the morning? And why should anyone care?

People don't buy what you do; they buy why you do it."

It is remarkable and powerful when a leader gets it right. Nick Sarillo of Nick's Pizza & Pub, an Illinois-based family dining business, shared his ideas with George.

> *" Your organization's purpose shapes behaviors, relationships, attitudes and the work environment. The purpose, "why" we do what we do, creates a meaningful place to work. The values are also important in creating an intentional culture because they are "how" we do the "what," whether it is pizza or widgets or accounting."*

Let's start with some definitions. Different people use these words in different ways. Here are ours:

Mission: Why we are here, why we exist, what business we are in.

Vision: Future picture—what we want to become, where we are going – in which others can envision themselves.

Objectives: Broadly defined, qualitative performance requirements.

Goals: The quantitative measures of the objectives that define success over a specific time period.

Values: The things you will not compromise on the way to delivering the mission and achieving the vision.

Guiding Principles: Expected actions flowing from values. From most to least directive:

- o **Policy:** A mandatory, definite course or method of action that all must follow. e.g. "Respond to all customer inquiries within 24 hours."

- o **Guideline:** A preferred course or method of action that all should generally follow. e.g. "Try to get back to all customers within 24 hours."

- o **Principle:** A way of thinking about actions. e.g. "Think customers first and pull in the people you need to answer customer inquiries right the first time as fast you can."

It's useful to deal with these in the context of purpose and happiness.

The Secret of Happiness

Happiness is good. Actually, there are three goods. Everyone strives for each of the three though each person weights them differently. (Some weight them very differently.) The three goods are:

1) Good for others
   - Meaning in the work (impact on others, match with values)
   - Share in shaping the destiny (influence, being informed)
2) Good at it
   - Match of activities with strengths and resources (support and time)
   - Employability (Learning, development, resume builder)
3) Good for me
   - Near term pleasure (enjoyable work/activities, fit with life interests)
   - Compensation (monetary, non-monetary reward, recognition, respect)

Link between happiness and purpose

As we've said, leadership is about inspiring, enabling and empowering others to do their absolute best together to realize a meaningful and rewarding shared purpose. Now we're suggesting that happiness is good: good for others; good at it; good for me. Cross the two:

> "Do their absolute best" is doing what people are good at.
> "Meaningful" is about good for others.
> "Rewarding" is about good for me.

Or, leadership is about inspiring, enabling and empowering others to do their absolute best together (good at it) to realize a meaningful (good for others) and rewarding (good for me) shared purpose. Happiness matters.

Mission: Why here, why exist, what business we are in.

Your mission is about beliefs. The most inspiring leaders have a passion for what they do. This cannot be replicated or forced. It oozes out of every pore, and others are attracted to that. People want to buy from people like this and work with people like this because they can see how much these people believe. BRAVE leaders flow their passion to the team so that everyone believes. BRAVE leaders won't stay in a position if they are not passionate, and recognize when it's time to move on.

While some mission statements can be flat, those with a strong belief behind them stand out. Simply put, a mission statement informs the organization of why it exists. The best mission statements are concise, clear, and motivating. They leave no question as to the "higher good", "good for others", or the "ultimate focus" of the organization. Your team should be able to apply the mission statement to everything they do. It should be so clear that they can relate it to any task.

A common mistake organizations make when crafting mission statements is making them so complex and convoluted that they fail to provide meaning for anyone. Keep them other-focused, pointed, accurate and inspiring. A few great mission statements:

> *"Provide relief to victims of disasters and help people prevent, prepare for, and respond to emergencies."* - American Red Cross
>
> *"Preserve and improve human life"* - Merck
>
> *"To explore new worlds, discover new civilizations; seek out new life forms, and to boldly go where no one has gone before."* - Starship Enterprise
>
> *"Provide a safe overnight shelter for the homeless and support services to help them achieve their highest level of self-sufficiency so that they might lead more fulfilling lives."* – adapted from Pacific House

These are so much more inspiring than:

> *"To increase shareholder value."*
>
> *"To be the most respected and admired market leader."*
>
> *"To meet our customers' needs."*

Mission Tool: Mission development is a journey of discovery versus creation. Your mission is dictated by others' needs. Often, it's handed to you. Other times you are called to it. Once you've made the choices around where to play and who to serve, the questions to ask are what do they need and why, and what must you deliver to meet those needs. Your mission flows from those.

Who needs us?

What do they need and why? (The problem they need solved.)

What must we deliver to meet their needs?

Thus, our mission:

 Note: Get this right. It's going to inform everything else you do. If you and your boss and your team are not clear on your mission, stop and get clear. Do not even try to do anything else until you are clear on why you are doing what you are doing.

Vision: Future picture—what we want to become, where we are going.

A good vision is an appealing picture of future success, showing what things will be like when the mission is accomplished. Some examples of clear and inspiring visions:

> *"The world's premier engineering organization. Trained and ready to provide support anytime, anyplace."* - U.S. Army Corps of Engineers

> *"Create a world renowned, yet personable, showcase of maverick films, filmmakers and the technology that enables creativity.* - Cinequest

> *"A world in which every child, everywhere, has equal access to life-saving vaccines."* - The Vaccine Fund

> *"A world without homelessness."* – Pacific House (adapted)

Critical point: the people the vision is designed to inspire must be able to picture themselves in the vision. Inspired members of the U.S. Army Corps of Engineers can see themselves trained and ready to provide support as part of the world's premier engineering organization. Inspired members of Cinequest can see themselves as part of a world renowned, yet personable showcase the enables creativity. Members of the Vaccine Fund can see themselves in a world in which every child, everywhere, has equal access to life-saving vaccines. These are rewarding pictures for these members.

TOOL 2.2
VISION

What will it look like when we achieve our mission?

Dreaming

One of Sinek's closing points in his TED talk was that Martin Luther King's great Washington talk was not the "I have a plan" talk. It was the "I have a dream" talk. A vision is a dream.

Gillian does an exercise with her team once a year to plan out five-year goals. She encourages them to dream big (many are afraid to do that.) She covers all aspects – Where will the company be? Who will our clients be? What roles will you have? What kinds of technologies will we be using? She makes sure they are as specific as possible. The first time she did this, some people thought she was crazy, but as the months went on and the team started ticking off some of the goals of year three in year one, they really got excited. They believed. Don't be afraid to dream – you never know where it can take you.

Carving out a vision with your team gets everyone on the same page. It comes from the team, not top down – which can be deflating. This is a critical component of inspiring others through points of inflection.

Often dreams from the top are very exciting and well intentioned, but there is a critical flaw – they don't align with middle management goals. Ensure that the vision is being supported at all levels of business.

Values: The things you will not compromise on the way to delivering the mission and achieving the vision.

If you choose to have a values-driven organization, the end does not justify the means. For these organizations, values are the bedrock upon which you build your culture. These are things you will not sacrifice even if it means the mission will fail.

Values may be words like these:
Company 1: Communication, Respect, Integrity, Excellence.
Company 2: Social Responsibility, Sustainability, Partnership, Volunteering.

Hard to argue with these words. Most of you would probably feel good working for organizations with values like these. Wrong. Company 1 was Enron. Company 2 was Volkswagen. Neither of these companies' leadership acted in line with their values. For them, the end justified the means. And that was their undoing. Enron is gone, leaving behind a trail of pain in its wake. Volkswagen's faking emission-testing results have severely if not mortally damaged its brand.

Guiding Principles: Expected actions flowing from values.

On the other hand, when Procter & Gamble bought Norwich Eaton, they dropped Charlie Carroll in as general manager. A little while after taking on the assignment, he visited the Norwich operation in Mexico. There he was presented with Norwich's leading drug – the number one selling drug in all of Mexico.

"What does it do?"

"It's a placebo. In your country doctors say 'take two aspirin and call me in the morning'. Here doctors have people take two of these and call them in the morning. It works half the time. And because it's a placebo, it has absolutely no side effects. Anyone can take it."

"Pull it off the market immediately."

Charlie didn't hesitate. Charlie didn't have to call anyone at headquarters to clear his decision. He knew that continuing to sell a placebo was in fundamental violation of Procter & Gamble's guiding principle of doing the right thing.

At one point another Procter & Gamble employee had presented P&G's VP of advertising, Richard Goldstein with what he thought was a tough choice. Richard didn't see it that way at all.

"Let's do this."

"But that will cost us business."

"Principles are only principles when they hurt."

This is the difference between hollow words on a wall and principles that actually guide choices. Don't misinterpret this. Personal values are important. Fit with personal values is the #1 thing New England Patriots' football coach Bill Belichick looks for in recruiting.[28] Personal values are bedrock. Guiding principles help turn those values into actions.

TOOL 2.3
VALUES AND GUIDING PRINCIPLES

What are the inviolate values in achieving our mission and vision?

How do those translate into guiding principles to guide actions?

[28] From George Bradt's February 1, 2018 Forbes.com article, "How to Apply Bill Belichick's Formula for Success to Your Business"

Perhaps get there with a shield exercise:

1. Each participant creates their own personal shield with the answers to some or all of the following in words, pictures, or a combination: Favorite: Person (hero,) Place (location,) Possession (thing you own,) Principles (that guide your behaviors,) Pastime (activity,) Present (gift,) Phantasy (dream for the future,) Source of pride (motivator)
2. Participants share their shields, explaining why they chose what they chose. Because…
3. Facilitator listens for and records values behind the choices.
4. Facilitator puts captured values on Post-it notes on wall.
5. Participants group values into clusters forming guiding principles – with verbs.

Another good approach we learned from a client is to ask people what incident they can think of that 'offended' your sense of who we are — the answer will indicate what you hold dear (aka, a value.)

Coherence

Mission, vision, values and guiding principles are different – but yours need to be congruent. If you run an organization that does assassinations for hire, it probably doesn't make sense to have preserving life as a core guiding principle. If you run an organization that is in the business of managing nuclear power plants once they are up and running, it probably doesn't make sense to have never doing things the same way twice as a guiding principle either.

How to Get People Actually to Follow Your Vision and Values[29]

People actually follow visions and values when they commit to them, see them turned into followable guiding principles, practice them consistently and have them reinforced. We've become so used to people's actions have so little in common with organizations' stated values that it's hardly even noteworthy when that happens. If job #1 for any CEO is to own the vision and values, they fail if people aren't following them. These four steps can make that happen.

---

[29] From George Bradt's April 24, 2018 Forbes.com article, "How to Get People to Actually Follow Your Vision and Values"

1) Commit to values

If you want your people to commit to your vision and values you need to let them co-create them. You're going to get the commitment you deserve. Tell and you'll get compliance. Invite contribution and you'll get contribution. Commitment requires real co-creation. If you can't do that, stop reading here and put tight controls in place because your people are going to do what they think they can away with.

2) Turn your values into followable guiding principles

Bill Belichick has this right. Recruit for values. Manage with guiding principles. Values are important. But they are ethereal. People may know they're good. But they don't know what to do with them. Guiding principles tell them what to do without the constraint of policies.

People happily working in an organization that values the team. They know what to do in an organization that guides them to commit to support and collaborate with each other. The closer you get to one over-arching guiding principle, the more likely people are to follow it.

3) Practice those value-based guiding principles consistently

> "We are what we repeatedly do. Excellence, then, is not an act, but a habit." — Will Durant

Commitment gives you desire. Guidelines gives you direction. Practice makes it stick.

Embed your values through guiding principles brought to life in your ADEPT talent practices (Acquire, Develop, Encourage, Plan, Transition.)

- Identify and recruit people who share your values and bring them onboard in a way that reflects your value-based guiding principles.
- Develop people in line with your guiding principles.
- Direct, resource, authorize, recognize and reward people in line with your guiding principles. The results they deliver matter. The way they deliver those results matters just as much.
- Take your guiding principles into account as you plan and transition people across, up or out.

Everything communicates. People will notice if these efforts follow or do not follow your guiding principles.

4) Reinforce your vision and values over and over again

As the CEO, owner, leader, you must own the vision and values. And you must own them all the time.

Atrium Health's President and CEO Gene Woods drives their mission "to improve health, elevate hope and advance healing, for all" all the time. He starts <u>every</u> meeting with what is known throughout the organization as a "Connect to Purpose." Every meeting. Every board meeting. Every leadership meeting. In fact, every gathering within in the organization begins in this same way. Different teammates and even invited guests are encouraged to highlight stories to remind themselves about what matters and remain connected to the positive impact they make.

You can see this in their annual report. It's full of stories like "Who is Madie DeBruhl?" (12-year-old bone marrow transplant patient.) Or "Who is Shelly Cooley?" (Nurse who goes well beyond the call of duty to help other people grow.) Or "Who is Lee Beatty?" (Family medicine physician who epitomizes how to "Deliver the gift of humanity.")

Over the past couple of years, I've worked with two companies where safety was paramount in the heavy manufacturing and coal mining space. Each of those companies started every meeting with a "Safety minute." Someone in the meeting had to share an idea or provide an update that would help everyone in the meeting be safe.

The Puritan cooking oil business was all about "healthy." George started every meeting by asking how that meeting was either going to make our consumers healthier or our business healthier. If people didn't know the answer, he walked out. People learned what they had to do to.

What you don't do communicates as much as what you do do. When John Pepper was passed over for CEO, he did not leave Procter & Gamble. Instead he supported the new CEO until it was his time. When Jalen Hurts went from Alabama's starting quarterback to back up, he kept his head in the game, supporting the team as required until it was his time.[30]

When it was their time, the people at Procter & Gamble and Alabama were eager to follow Pepper and Hurts to new heights. Their actions and inactions had proved they were other-focused leaders.

---

[30] From George Bradt's December 2, 2018 Forbes.com article, "Leadership Mindset Lessons From Alabama Football's Sabin, Tagovailoa And Hurts"

Be. Do. Say. The Foundation of Authentic, Trusted Leadership[31]

In their town, deep in the last century, the paramedics and emergency medical technicians that staffed the life squad's ambulance were volunteers. They were on call for twelve-hour shifts and carried beepers so they could be summoned whatever they were doing.

He was on call and at home when he heard an accident on the corner.

He ran down to see if people needed help and he found a two-car accident. So, he secured the victims as best he could, got some bystanders to put one of the victims in traction, and got others to call the police and life squad and tell them he was on site and needed help.

When the rest of the life squad showed up, they packaged up the victims, safely transported them to the hospital and returned to the life squad building to clean the ambulance and restock it for its next call.

The life squad captain walked in and addressed him.

"I noticed you were on the scene of that accident without your red jacket on."

"Yes. I was. I had been at home, working in my front yard. I heard the accident and ran straight there to help as quickly as I could. I leave my jacket in my car when I'm on duty."

"I understand. But you should take the extra time and get your jacket. Its visibility helps keep you safe on site and helps you control the scene."

"You're absolutely right. My mistake. Won't do it again."

He turned to go back to his work.

Then he stopped.

"How did you notice I was on the scene without my jacket?"

"I drove by."

"I'm sorry. You drove by the scene of a two-car accident close enough and slowly enough to notice that I wasn't wearing my jacket? You must have noticed that I was the only one on the scene. I could have used some help."

Let's be clear on this, the captain was right to enforce the jacket policy. Her

---

[31] From George Bradt's October 20, 2020 Forbes article "*Be. Do. Say. The Foundation of Authentic, Trusted Leadership*"

logic made total sense. The issue was that her actions were not in line with the squad's mission. Every life squad there ever was and ever will be has had and will have a mission of providing emergency medical care.

In an earlier article on the Red Cross's Charley Shimanski, we looked at his story of people in a restaurant who hear the sound of a significant car accident. As he describes it,

- Many will go to the window to see what happened.

- Some will go to the curb to see what happens next.

- But a small number of those patrons will rush to the accident scene to BE what happens next - helping out however they can to the best of their abilities.

The Red Cross are second responders. They support first responders and victims. Life Squads are first responders. Their mission is to "rush to the accident scene to BE what happens next – helping out however they can to the best of their abilities."

Implications for you

Not suggesting you have to rush to accident scenes – unless you're the captain of a life squad. But your actions must match your words and your underlying beliefs if you're going to have any credibility as a leader.

No one's going to believe your words, what you say. Talk is cheap.

People will believe what you do.

Pick your cliché. Walk the talk. Practice what you preach. That's table stakes. But if your actions match your words without matching your fundamental underlying beliefs, you will slip up and you will get caught.

Be. Do. Say. Starts with "Be." Make sure you truly believe in your organization's mission and values. If you do, it's easy to talk about it. Just say what comes naturally. If you do, let your actions flow from those underlying beliefs.

If you don't fundamentally believe in your organization's mission, get out. There may be some short-term benefits to staying for a while. You may be able to learn new things. You may be able to practice new skills. You may get valuable recognition and rewards.

But you can't be the best leader you can be unless everything about you inspires, enables and empowers others to do their absolute best together to realize a meaningful and rewarding shared purpose. You'll drive by accidents until you're the accident yourself.

Summary: What Matters and Why

Get the team aligned around a coherent shared purpose:

- **Mission**: Why we are here, why we exist, what business we are in.
- **Vision**: Future picture—what we want to become, where we are going – in which others can envision themselves.
- **Values**: The things you will not compromise on the way to delivering the mission and achieving the vision.
- **Guiding Principles:** Expected actions flowing from values.
    - **Policy:** A mandatory, definite course or method of action that all must follow.
    - **Guideline:** A preferred course or method of action that all should generally follow.
    - **Principle:** A way of thinking about actions.

Make sure you and your key stakeholders are aligned around objectives and goals and the timing for delivery of those goals. Understand that owners of public companies may have a bias to look at quarterly and annual results. Private equity owners may care about value creation in their fund's lifespan. Family owners may care about generational wealth creation.

Once you define what matters, what the end game is at the other side of the point of inflection, and once the team buys in, decisions become more straightforward, (sometimes even in hard times.) **

3 *Attitude*: Make Choices Around Overarching Strategy, Priorities, and Culture

This chapter gets at the choices driving how leaders and their teams will win – strategy, priorities and culture. Like your mission, vision, and guiding principles, these need to form a coherent whole.

Let's start by defining the terms:

- **Strategy**: The single overarching choice
- **Strategic priorities, enablers, and capabilities:** in line with that
- **Culture:** Behaviors, relationships, attitudes, values, environment

Strategic planning is about generating and selecting options to close gaps between objectives and current realities. It is about the creation and allocation of resources to the right place, in the right way, at the right time, over time to overcome barriers and deliver what matters.

Michael Porter suggests that almost any value chain includes design/invention, production, delivery, and customer service/experience in addition to marketing and selling. Your single overarching strategy should identify the right way to build and leverage differentially valuable advantages versus competitors at one of the first four while also marketing and selling – which every organization must do one way or another.

Strategic Priorities focus people on the most important areas.

Hardware and Software Enablers like systems & processes, infrastructure (data/technology/ IT/ security, operational including procurement and supply chain, organizationally/HR, financial reporting/tax/accounting/ compliance, new product development,) balance sheet & cash flows (modernization and growth-oriented capital spending, back office) enable delivery of priorities.

Organizational Capabilities across senior leadership (Commercial, Operations, Technology/IT, Finance, HR, Legal, R&D, M&A,) middle management and individual and team strengths including project management/transformation are those required for the enablers to work.

The critical resource allocation choice is where to

- *Win* by being: Predominant/top 1%, Superior/top 10%, Strong/top 25%
- *Not lose* by being: Above average/competitive, Good enough/scaled, or
- *Not do* by: Outsourcing or not doing at all.

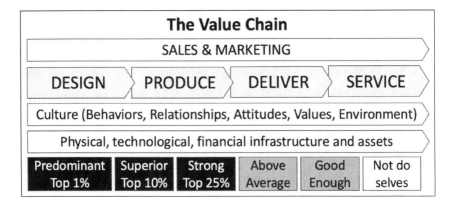

The Value Chain

SALES & MARKETING			
DESIGN	PRODUCE	DELIVER	SERVICE
Culture (Behaviors, Relationships, Attitudes, Values, Environment)			
Physical, technological, financial infrastructure and assets			

Predominant Top 1%	Superior Top 10%	Strong Top 25%	Above Average	Good Enough	Not do selves

Not all should be proactive. Certainly design-focused organizations like Apple must be. But organizations like Coca-Cola are better off as fast-followers taking others' ideas and scaling them. Walmart is all about coordination. And the Ritz prides itself on responsive and agile service.

Plank:	Design	Produce	Deliver	Service
Example:	Apple	Coca-Cola	Walmart	Ritz-Carlton
Manner:	Proactive	Fast-follow	Coordinated	Responsive
Culture:	Independent	Stable	Interdependent	Flexible

For example, leveraging service as a strategic advantage requires the right mindset. Only organizations with a "service first" mentality can even hope to create a service advantage. But that's not enough. You must combine that with the right service framework like Clicksoftware CEO Moshe BenBassat's W6 questions: *Who does what for whom with what where and when?*[32]

On one level, BenBassat's W6 merely take basic milestone management up a notch beyond *what is getting done by whom when*. However, when it comes to service delivery you do need more than basics. While manufacture planning concerns scheduling machines and materials, service planning requires more sophisticated time management and skill optimization.

BenBassat's first "aha moment" was sparked by his work helping the Israeli air force assemble its annual schedule. The existing process involved *"putting four smart officers in a room and not letting them out until they had a solution"* to optimize planes, fuel, exercises, and people's time. This took months, literally. Instead, BenBassat built a software solution which leveraged artificial intelligence to do what the officers did – but in minutes.

[32] George Bradt on Forbes.com February 13, 2013

We'll leave it to BenBassat to explain the software, focusing here on applying BenBassat's W6 logic to your service planning, regardless of the problem you are trying to solve.

1. **For Whom?**

Begin with the client of your service. This is another form of the BRAVE leadership question, "Where to play?" Note that the more demanding customers are not necessarily the highest priority. "First come first served" and "The squeakiest wheel gets oiled first" are not value-creating strategies.

2. **What?**

With the client in mind, get clear on what services you are going to provide – and not provide.

3. **Who?**

Service is delivered by people with unequal skills. As BenBassat experienced in his work with utility companies, the skills required to install are different than those required to repair. Find the person with the right skills and temperament to deliver the specific service required.

4. **With What?**

Service requires resources. We've all experienced plumbers assessing a problem and then leaving to retrieve the required parts. To properly leverage service, ensure your people have the tools and materials they need when they need them.

5. **Where?**

There's been a fundamental shift in where some services are delivered. Sometimes it still makes sense to go where the need is (e.g. doctor house calls.) Other times, it's better to have the need brought to you (e.g. hospital operations.) Make a considered choice.

6. When?

Not all service requires immediate delivery and delivering ASAP is expensive. In many instances, the monetary cost advantages in batching service delivery outweigh the customer satisfaction cost of delay.

BenBassat's W6 *Who does what for whom with what where and when?* is a valuable framework which can be used to leverage service as a strategic weapon – especially if one combines discipline with the right attitude in terms of strategy, priorities and culture.

And in today's competitive economy, where many companies can no longer rely on product or pricing as a differentiator, it is the service experience that is influencing buying decisions.

Think through which manner is appropriate for the strategy you and your team have chosen.

Innovation Follow Through – Richard Branson

Richard Branson has achieved remarkable success taking the Virgin brand into industries "*out of frustration*" with existing record, airline, and telecommunication companies and the like. He looks for "obvious gaps in the market" and launches products or services that are "*heads above everyone else.*" To continue to succeed (in industries that don't "*get killed by a technological change*") he says "*The way you survive is to be much more creative than your rivals.*"

It's one of Branson's main themes. As he said in a recent graduation speech[33] "*We always enter markets where the leaders are not doing a great job, so we can go in and disrupt them by offering better quality services.*" Now he's so tired of waiting for NASA that he's launching his own space travel program. This is definitely a man who reaches for the stars over and over again.

For Branson, it's about being "*much more creative than our rivals*" (design.) For others it's about producing better or delivering better, or providing superior customer service. You and your team need to figure out the strategy for how you are going to win.

---

[33] Posted on LinkedIn May 21, 2013

Competing with Industry Giants? Five Keys to Winning in the Niches[34]

When the elephants fight, the grass suffers (African proverb.) Don't pick a fight with the elephants of your industry. Don't play in the field where they are fighting. You don't need the elephants to lose for you to win. You just need to avoid getting trampled. And you need to think through five essentials: Conditions, Customers, Competitors, Collaborators, Capabilities.

Elke Goversten did this well at parenting magazine, Mamalode. As a small player in a declining industry Elke knew her organization's survival depended upon avoiding the wrath of the big players. Elke told me it was all about *"focus and flexibility"* while choosing to *"only exist in a business model that was as meaningful as our product."*

She went on to say, *"If we don't know what to do, we do the opposite of the big guys."* In particular, they flipped the platform from writers writing on the Mamalode platform to Mamalode publishing on writers' platforms and *"developing models to scale print in a meaningful way in collaboration with print partners like hospitals."* Their growth came from their ability to leverage other platforms that the big players in their industry hadn't even considered.

This was a classic case of Zigging when your competitors Zagged. Worst choice: compete with industry giants head-to-head with commodity products. Better choice: differentiate into product niches the giants either don't care about or can't compete in – or even better, follow Mamalode's example down the path to differentiated, protectable business models.

Think in terms of: Conditions, Customers, Competitors, Collaborators, Capabilities.

Conditions

Those that put customers first don't survive against industry giants. Why? Because that's exactly what the industry giants do. Going there means direct competition with those giants – where you will get trampled like grass.

---

[34] From George Bradt's December 17, 2014 Forbes.com article, "Competing with Industry Giants? Five Keys to Winning in the Niches"

Instead, dig into social and demographic trends, political, governmental and regulatory fronts, macro and micro economic trends, and market definitions including inflows, outflows and substitutes.

Customers

Then turn to customers. If the industry giants are already serving all the needs of all the potential customers and doing it well, give up. Go play somewhere else. But there is most likely a gap in the market. Not all of us can do what Tony Hsieh did and find an industry in shambles like the retail shoe industry creating the opportunity for Zappos, but you should be able to find some unmet or underserved needs.

By the way, that unmet or underserved need could be anywhere along the value chain from first line customers to end users to influencers. Dig into their needs, hopes, preferences, commitments, strategies and price/value perspectives.

Competitors

Having looked at customers and potential customers, examine your competitors. You can't stay out of the way of the giants without knowing where they are and anticipating where they are going. Reconstruct their strategies, profit/value models, profit pools by segment and source of pride. Know that if you attack what they hold dear, they will come after you. The objective is to carve out something they don't care about so it's in their best interest to ignore you.

But don't ignore the rest of the industry. This includes other players and other potential players. You're looking for blue oceans, not just smaller blood baths.

Collaborators

Collaborators are those that will benefit from your success. These could be suppliers, business allies, partners, government/community leaders. In an industry dominated by giants, the balance of power is skewed. Look for collaborators suffering under the pressure. They can help you find and build a niche.

Capabilities

With all those in mind you can now turn your attention to building the capabilities you'll need to win in your chosen niche. Look across human, operational, financial, technical and asset dimensions to build only what you need, outsourcing the rest so you can stay focused and flexible.

A Six-Step Strategic Planning Process

The following six-step process will allow you to create a complete and robust strategic plan. We are not suggesting that this is the only way to do this. But it is a good way.

1. Set an aspirational destination (derived from the mission, vision and values/guiding principles.)

2. Assess the current reality and develop potential future scenarios.

3. Identify options to bridge gaps between the current reality and the desired aspiration.

4. Evaluate options under different scenarios. Make choices.

5. Develop detailed plans that will deliver on selected priorities.

6. Act, measure, adjust, and repeat.

Set the Aspirational Destination

Strategic planning begins with the aspirational long-term destination, which should be derived directly from the mission, vision, and guiding principles. It is important for this step to come before looking at the current reality. Starting with the current reality tends to limit thinking and produce incremental results. Starting with the end in mind encourages bigger ideas.

Assess the Current Reality and Develop Future Scenarios

But the next step is to analyze the current reality. This involves reviewing, once again, the 5Cs (Customers, Collaborators, Capabilities, Competitors, and Conditions) as well as performing a SWOT (Strengths, Weaknesses, Opportunities, Threats) analysis.

Developing scenarios is an exercise in trying to foresee potential changes in the environment (social, political, demographic, organizational, economic, etc.) that might impact your strategic choices. The changes are generally outside the control of the organization or the team – particularly in today's volatile, uncertain, complex and ambiguous (VUCA) era of ever-accelerating technological change. Given this, the organization cannot choose which scenario will happen; but it can estimate the probabilities of each scenario happening. This can help determine the expected results of different strategic options.

Identify Options to Bridge Gaps between Reality and Aspiration

Next, determine what strategic options might create additional value (or in some cases, minimize its destruction.) Be creative, thinking out of the box so you can come up with a range of options perhaps building on your key leverage points (offensively) and key business issues (defensively). And be bold in line with McKinsey's research[35] that most meaningful value is created by one of five moves:

- Resource reallocation;
- Programmatic mergers, acquisitions and divestitures;
- Capital expenditure;
- Productivity improvements;
- Differentiation improvements

(at least 30% more than the industry median for the last three)

This is a good time to get stakeholder input. You are trying to generate ideas. So, if your stakeholders have good ideas, you want to know about them. At this stage, make sure everyone understands that you are not looking for decisions, just input and options.

Evaluate Options under Different Scenarios

In this step determine which options create the most risk-adjusted value over time, under different scenarios. Evaluate options and scenarios leading to a range of forecasts based on transparent assumptions. At this point, involve key stakeholders to understand and to help improve the components of the valuation assumptions.

For example, assume three scenarios for the future of the industry:

1. Industry consolidation: Number of customers shrinking.
2. Industry stagnation: Number of customers constant.
3. Industry expansion: Number of customers increasing.

To determine which of your options has the highest expected value, figure out what the payoff will be under each scenario and what the probabilities will be of each happening.

Eventually get the key stakeholders involved to agree on which option to pursue.

---

[35] McKinsey – The Mindsets and Practices of Excellent CEOs Octoberr 25, 2019

After a complete evaluation, make the choices defining where the organization will focus its efforts and how it will win versus its competition. Aim to have one single overarching strategy and three to five strategic priorities that will deliver 75 percent of the goals.

Develop Detailed Business Plans

With those choices in place, develop detailed operational and organizational business plans for each priority. For each, clarify: 1) Direction - objectives, intent, interdependencies, 2) Resources – in line with priority choices, 3) Bounded authority - decision-making, RACI, ways of working, 4) Accountabilities - how track, measure, report

Don't underestimate the importance of timing. You must build capabilities to deliver the programs required to move from your current reality to a different destination. If you focus on only the programs, you won't have the capabilities to implement them (path I). If you overinvest in building capabilities, you'll run out of cash (path III). The art is in mapping out and implementing a carefully timed, stepped approach (path II)

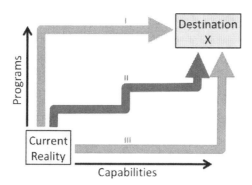

Act, Measure, Adjust, and Repeat

Once the detailed business plan is in play continually monitor its progress against your stated goals to ensure what you thought would happen is happening in a timely manner.

To ensure that the team members remain on target to get to their aspirational destination:

Get milestones in place immediately.

Track them and manage them as a team on a frequent and regular basis. Don't underestimate the power of celebrating early wins.

Adjust as necessary.

This whole process is about you and your team working together. Your team must feel like they're a part of the process but so too must your key stakeholders. Remember to include your stakeholders by:

- Obtaining their input to enhance scenarios and options. Engage with them and capture their ideas.
- Involving them to help understand and to improve valuation assumptions. Tap into their experience and context.
- Gaining their agreement on which options to pursue. (This should naturally occur as a result of the expected valuation of different options under different scenarios.)

Strategic Planning Summary

Your overarching strategy guides how to play in the right way to the organization's unique strengths relative to its competitors at one plank on the value chain: design, produce, deliver, or service. This requires clarity around choices on the proactive – fast-follow – coordination – reactive continuum.

Strategic planning begins with the aspirational destination that is drawn from the vision and mission:

Analyze the current reality by using the 5Cs approach.

Complete a SWOT summary.

Create strategy options to guide actions, overcome barriers, and bridge gaps.

Get key stakeholder input into options and assumptions.

Get key stakeholder agreement on which overarching strategy and strategic priorities to pursue when.

Develop business plans with operational and organizational actions that are needed to implement each selected option.

Tool 3.1
Strategic Planning

Input: Mission | vision | value proposition | guiding principles (core nature)
         Situation assessment/SWOT | profit pools | where to play choices

1. – Set or reconfirm the aspirational destination/ambition (flows from mission, vision, and guiding principles)

2. – Assess the current reality (from situation assessment/SWOT and profit pools) and develop possible future scenarios:
    Base/most likely scenario:
    Optimistic scenario:
    Pessimistic scenario:

3. – Generate strategic options to bridge gaps between reality and aspiration
    Strategic option 1
    Strategic option 2
    Strategic option 3

    ⇨ Peer and management input to enhance scenarios and options

4. Evaluate strategic options under different scenarios and make choices

    ⇨ Peer and management involvement to understand and improve valuation assumptions.

    ⇨ Management agreement on which overarching strategy and strategic priorities to pursue when.

5. – Develop detailed business plans

6. – Act, measure, adjust/improve, and repeat

Copyright© PrimeGenesis®. To customize this document, download Tool 3.1 from the BRAVE Leadership page on www.onboardingtools.com.

The business planning tool (Tool 3.2) is closely related to the strategic planning tool, putting more detail on some of the elements. Use the two tools together.

Strategic Plan

Destination: Mission, Vision, Objectives, Goals

Strategy:

> *Plank:* (Design, Produce, Deliver or Service [all must Sell])
>
> *Posture:* (Shape/Proactive, Adapt/Fast-follow, Reserve/Prepare-Resp.)
>
> *Culture:* (e.g. Independence, Stability, Interdependence, Flexibility)
>
> *Overarching strategy:*

Strategic Priorities/Resource allocation:

> (e.g. Predominant/top 1%, Superior/top 10%, Strong/top 25%,
>
> Above average/top 50%, Good enough/scale, not do/ally/outsource)

Rules of engagement across critical business drivers

Resource Plan (requirements, application, sources)

> Human
>
> Financial
>
> Physical
>
> Technical
>
> Operational

Action Plan

	Actions	Timing	Responsibilities	Linkages
Near-term				
Long-term				

Performance Management Plan

> Operating and financial performance standards
>
> Management Cadence
>
> > *Annual* (Strategic, Organizational, Operational processes)
> >
> > *Quarterly* (Business Reviews):
> >
> > *Monthly* (Programs):
> >
> > *Weekly* (Projects):
> >
> > *Daily* (Tasks):
> >
> > (More frequently in a crisis)

Culture

US Army colonel Randy Chase spent ten days on a navy ship for cross training. On his second day, he ran out of toothpaste so he went over to the ship's store to buy another tube. The stores on navy ships aren't as big as your typical suburban supermarket (only two people could fit in the store at a time,) so there was a short line to get in. He went to the end of the line and said "good morning" to the man in front of him who took one look at him and ran away. Almost immediately, a navy lieutenant appeared and asked "Colonel sir. What are you doing?"

What had he done wrong?

Colonel Chase had done two things wrong. At that time (1) Officers didn't talk to enlisted men on ships except to convey orders. (2) Officers didn't wait in lines.

True. True. This incident took place in the last century. But the cultural differences between the services are still there. As Boris Groysberg, Andrew Hill, and Toby Johnson describe in "Which of These People Is Your Future CEO?" in the November 2010 Harvard Business Review, the navy and air force are strong on process and light on flexibility, while the army and marines are lighter on process and stronger on flexibility. They argue these differences stem from the toys with which the different services play. A small mistake on a ship can have devastating impact, as can not reacting to a changing situation in ground warfare.

There are some deep-seated cultural differences in organizations that have their roots in the context in which those organizations operate. It's important for leaders to understand what drives behaviors, relationships and attitudes before trying to fight them or change them.

This matters – a lot. Gallup looks at the link between culture, employee engagement and business results on a regular basis. They note organizations with the most engaged employees have 41% less absenteeism and 24% less turnover, are +17% more productive, resulting in +10% higher customer ratings, +20% more sales, and +21% more profits[36].

---

[36] Jim Harter and Annamarie Mann, *The Right Culture: Not Just About Employee Satisfaction,* Workplace, April 12, 2017

An organization's culture underpins "The way we do things here" and is made up of BRAVE Behaviors, Relationships, Attitudes, Values, and Environment. Just as an individual has preferences, so, too, does an organization. The BRAVE cultural framework and tool will help you a) understand the existing organizational preferences, and b) evolve them in a coherent fashion.

When it comes to culture, use dimensions like these.[37] (This is one of those areas to adapt for your specific situation.)

Environment:
Office Layout: Hierarchical/closed/walled
  vs. Collaborative/open
Office Décor/Dress: Formal (coats and ties)
  vs. Casual (jeans and tee-shirts)
Facilities: Work-focused (offices and conference rooms)
  vs. Work-life integration (Ping-pong, foosball, casual sitting areas)

Values
Purpose: More apt to follow purpose rigidly as written
  vs. flexibly as intended
Learning: More rigidly following learning direction
  vs. flexibly, openly sharing
Results: Results (Achievement driven, goal focused)
  vs. Caring (Warm, sincere, relational)

Attitude:
Strategy: More driving minimum viable product at lowest possible cost
  vs. innovating to create more value for customers.
Manner: More responsive to requests
  vs. proactively doing things ahead of being asked.
Safety: Safety (Realistic, careful, prepared)
  vs. Learning (Open, inventive, exploring)

[37] Partly pulled from The Leader's Guide to Corporate Culture by Boris Groysberg, Jeremiah Lee, Jesse Price, and J. Yo-Jud Cheng, Harvard Business Review Jan/Feb 2018

Relationships:

Decisions: More hierarchical and structured

vs. diffused and flexible

Communication: More formal, written, structured

vs. more informal, verbal, flexible

Authority: Authority (Bold, decisive, dominant)

vs. Purpose (Purpose driven, idealistic, tolerant)

Behaviors:

Discipline: More structured

vs. more fluid/flexible

Unit: Independent (on own, work groups)

vs. Interdependent (teams)

Order: Order (Rule abiding, respectful, cooperative)

vs. Enjoyment (Playful, instinctive, fun loving)

Not surprisingly, when you apply these criteria to the army you get a very different picture than you do with the navy. It's not that one is better than the other. It's just that they are different – as should be the culture in the operating room and disease diagnosing rooms of the same hospital.

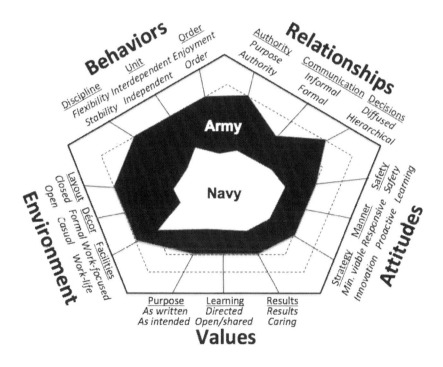

People generally learn about culture starting with the most superficial (what people say about their culture,) but it is rooted in what people really are, their core assumptions and beliefs. "Be. Do. Say." This approach can be applied to people individually and to organizations on a whole. Let's take a deeper look at each element.

Be: The underpinning of culture (and integrity) is what people really are, their core assumptions, beliefs, and intentions. These show up in attitudes and principle-guided behaviors.

Do: These are behavioral, attitudinal, and communication norms that can be seen, felt, or heard such as signs and symbols like physical layouts, the way people dress, talk to each other, and interact with each other. These show up in behaviors, relationships, and the work environment.

Say: What people say about their culture can be found in things like mission statements, creeds, and stories. As Edgar Schein points out, these get at the professed culture.[38]

For a culture to be sustainable, the BRAVE elements and what people say, do, and are must be in sync. It is easy to see when people's behaviors don't match their words. It is far more difficult to figure out when their words and behaviors match each other, but don't match underlying values. Yet, when that happens, those people's behaviors, relationships, and attitudes will change over time. Just as your own values, actions, and words need to line up, the same is true for those of an organization.

BRAVE Tip   Look well beyond the professed culture: It's not what people like about their preferences. It's just that value statements and creeds are often aspirational. You must understand the resting, steady state norms of behaviors, relationships, attitudes, values, and the work environment that people default to "when the boss is not around."

According to True Value's former CEO Lyle Heidemann, changing a corporate culture is a five-year effort. He also said that it doesn't seem to work well to attack behaviors or relationships head on. It's very hard to evolve values quickly, and generally speaking it is expensive to change the environment. That leaves attitude.

---

[38] See Edgar Schein, Organizational Culture and Leadership (San Francisco: Jossey-Bass, 1985.)

Implications for you:

1. Start with the cause, the why. Get all aligned around your purpose. Make sure all believe in its import and are committed to a common vision

2. Reconfirm where to play choices, within the ever-changing environmental context

3. Reconfirm the organization's core values, trying to change them only if absolutely necessary

4. Then adjust your attitude, relooking at strategic priorities, priorities, and culture and how they sync

5. Once everyone understands the attitudinal choices, relook at relationships and behaviors through that lens, evolving them as dictated by the new attitude

TOOL 3.3
CULTURE ASSESSMENT

Environment – *Where play*
OFFICE LAYOUT
Hierarchical/closed   1 – 2 – 3 – 4 – 5   Collaborative/open

OFFICE DÉCOR/DRESS
Formal   1 – 2 – 3 – 4 – 5   Casual

FACILITIES
Work-focused   1 – 2 – 3 – 4 – 5   Work-life integration

Other observations:

Values – *What matters*
PURPOSE
As written   1 – 2 – 3 – 4 – 5   As intended

LEARNING
Directed   1 – 2 – 3 – 4 – 5   Open/shared

RESULTS
Results   1 – 2 – 3 – 4 – 5   Caring

Underlying beliefs:

Attitude – *How Win*
STRATEGY
Min. viable prod.   1 – 2 – 3 – 4 – 5   Innovation

MANNER
Responsive   1 – 2 – 3 – 4 – 5   Proactive

SAFETY
Safety   1 – 2 – 3 – 4 – 5   Learning

Other observations:

Relationships – *How Connect*

DECISIONS
Hierarchical   1 – 2 – 3 – 4 – 5   Diffused

COMMUNICATION
Formal   1 – 2 – 3 – 4 – 5   Informal

AUTHORITY
Authority   1 – 2 – 3 – 4 – 5   Purpose

Other observations:

Behaviors – *What Impact*

DISCIPLINE
Stability   1 – 2 – 3 – 4 – 5   Flexibility

UNIT
Independent   1 – 2 – 3 – 4 – 5   Interdependent

ORDER
Order   1 – 2 – 3 – 4 – 5   Enjoyment

Other observations:

The Art of Losing Well So You Can Win Later[39]

Show me a good loser – and I'll show you a loser. As Tom Brady said after the Patriots dismantled the Chargers and before beating the Chiefs in overtime to get to their third Super Bowl in a row, "I just like winning." Who doesn't? Still, there is an art to losing well. It's all about accepting defeat, living your principles, and finding new ways to win the next time.

You all have your favorite examples. Some involve armies, sports, or leaders like Russia's retreating battles, the remarkable turnaround of the German national soccer team, or Steve Jobs.

Russia and Winter

Sometimes you have to lose a bunch of battles to win the war. Russia epitomized this when invaded by Napoleon and then Hitler. They kept losing. They kept retreating. Eventually Napoleon and then Hitler outran their supply lines and succumbed to Russia's brutal winter as history repeated itself.

They aren't the only nation or nation-formers to do something like this. George Washington lost battle after battle until he trapped the British army at Yorkville. A couple of centuries later, the British army's escape from Dunkirk preserved it for eventual victory in World War II.

German National Soccer Team

The roots of Germany's 2014 World Cup Win were planted right after their 1998 quarter final loss to Croatia. Germany had been a perennial powerhouse. But they had stopped investing in youth soccer. After their humiliating defeat they recommitted to your soccer through local clubs. They also committed to changing their style of play from individuals doing their jobs to building a team committed to winning together. The stars of their 2014 team were the first brought up in the new systems.

---

[39] From George Bradt's January 21, 2019 Forbes.com article, "The Art of Losing Well So You Can Win Later"

Development, hunger, and belief. We've seen that play out over and over again. Think about the "Miracle" team. 1969 Mets? 1980 US hockey team? How about Leicester City's one-year turnaround from near relegation to premier league champions under Claudio Ranieri. One colleague succinctly identified the ingredients to that as the resources they needed to win, an attitude of winning, and playing to win as a team.

Steve Jobs

There are few more humiliating defeats than getting fired from the company you founded. As most of the world knows, Steve Jobs went away, kept innovating, built a couple of other companies including Pixar and returned to lead Apple to become the most valuable company in the world for a while.

Other examples. Peter Cuneo took Marvel Comics from near death into the powerhouse of Marvel Entertainment. Michael Eisner and Frank Wells took over a dying Disney and revitalized its animation engine, theme park revenues, property management and retail. Reed Hastings recovered from the disaster of spinning off Qwikster with separate revenue streams for streaming and direct mail to build the base of today's Netflix. Abraham Lincoln lost every election but one.

Implications

Accept Defeat

You can't lose well without losing. Failing fast is relatively easy when it's a small-scale test. The bigger the impact, the harder it is to call the game. Too many manage downsides on the way to an ultimate failure, prolonging the agony and doing ever more damage along the way with a death by thousand cuts. Don't do that. Know when to switch from rescue to recovery.

Live Your Principles

If your guiding principles are the things you choose to follow even if you must go out of business, then follow them in defeat. If you say your customers or constituents or people matter most, take care of them when it hurts most and matters most.

Find New Ways to Win

This is about residual value. Having accepted defeat and honored your principles, Start anew, recovering and rebuilding off your strengths whether those are Russia's environment, Germany's youth, Jobs' innovations, or your secret sauce.

Accept that your <u>best current thinking</u> is not good enough. You lost. Now, update that thinking. Re-look at your situation. Re-check your ambitions. Find a new way to leverage your strengths to win.

Lose well now. Win the next time around.

Summary: How to Win

- Clarify strategy generating and selecting options that will close the gaps between the objectives and current reality
- Clarify your one and only single strategy to guide everything else.
- Lay out strategic priorities (in line with the single strategy,) enablers of those priorities, and the capabilities required to deliver the enablers.
- Make resource choices across your strategic priorities, enablers, and capabilities in order to:
  - Win by being: Predominant/top 1%, Superior/top 10%, Strong/top 25%
  - Not lose by being: Above average/competitive, Good enough/scaled, or
  - Not do by: Outsourcing or not doing at all.
- Choose your BRAVE culture across behaviors, relationships, attitudes, values and environment.
- Make sure your strategy, priorities, and culture reinforce each other.
- Lose well by accepting defeat, living your principles, and finding new ways to win the next time. **

4 *Relationships*: The Heart of Leadership

The most important moments of impact involve one human being connecting with another human being. The relationship could be emotionally charged, direct, or indirect. Either way, what you've thought through and done before sets up the moment of impact and what happens afterwards.

Setting up, managing, and following through from those moments of impact well requires a tremendous amount of thinking and work. Thus, this is our longest chapter. It could be overwhelming. So, we've broken it into a section on communication frameworks and then people leadership.

In many ways, this is the heart of inspiring, enabling and empowering others.

As Carl Buehner put it:

> *"People will forget what you said, people will forget what you did, but people will never forget how you made them feel."*[40]

Let's begin by putting in place some frameworks for communication.

Engagement: Compliant – Contributing - Committed

Crossing the secret of happiness (good for others, good at it, good for me, as outlined in Chapter 2) and Maslow's hierarchy of needs produces a way to look at different levels of engagement: compliant, contributing, committed.

Compliant - At the first level of engagement, compliant people do no harm. They show up. They observe. They focus on what's "good for me" and meet the minimum requirements to satisfy their biological and physiological needs. They want jobs.

Contributing - One level up, contributors do things they are "good at." They collaborate with others and help as they seek belonging and self-esteem. They want careers.

Committed - At the highest level are those seeking to do "good for others." They care about the organization's purpose and teach others as part of their own self-actualization. They have callings.

---

[40] *Richard Evans' Quote Book*, 1971, Publisher's Press (Note the poet Maya Angelou later paraphrased this and many attribute it to her.)

Communication Levels: Emotional – Direct – Indirect

Moving people through from disengaged to compliant to contributing to committed requires different levels of communication.

Indirect communication can build awareness and enough understanding for people to be able to comply with requests and direction to do their jobs.

Direct communication can build the understanding that enables people to make active contributions and forward their careers.

Emotional communication can change what people believe and how they feel as part of inspiring their commitment to an idea, cause or calling.

Persuasion

Bryan Smith lays out different ways of persuading people in a section in *The Fifth Discipline Fieldbook*[41]: tell – sell – test – consult – co-create. We have found that

Telling someone to do something yields compliance at best.

Selling, testing, and consulting sets people up to contribute.

Co-creating is one of the best ways to engender commitment.

Self-awareness

Communication begins with self-awareness. Some thoughts on this:

- You can't lead until you know yourself.
- Know how your communication style affects others.
- Recognize different styles in others, and pull out their strengths.

With self-awareness comes self-confidence. Self-aware beings are assured of their decisions; they are aware of their strengths as well as their weaknesses so they are confident, but not arrogant. When this type of self-aware confidence shines through, others will follow.

---

[41] from The Fifth Discipline Fieldbook, Peter Senge et al, Nicholas Brealey Publishing, London, 1994

Honest, open, vulnerable two-way communication is the foundation of successful relationships, both in business and in our personal lives. Excel at communicating with different styles.

Communication is not a one-time event. To change how people feel, think in terms of a communication MAP - Message, Amplifiers, Perseverance.

Message

Frame your message by thinking through the platform for change, vision, and call to action. Then distill those components down to one driving organizing concept, message and key communication points. Your organizing concept is the strategic core idea you execute in your message and communication points to impact how others feel.

No one will do anything different until they a) believe they must change, b) can picture themselves in a brighter future, and c) see how they can be part of the solution.

> **Platform for change -** The things that will make your audience realize they need to do something different than what they have been doing.

> **Vision -** Picture of a brighter future—in which your audience can picture themselves.

> **Call to action -** Actions the audience can take to get there.

To illustrate these points, imagine a pack of polar bears. They are playing on an ice flow. It's melting! It's drifting out to sea! The bears either are going to drown or starve to death. Neither scenario is good. [Platform for change] However there is some food nearby sitting on land. The bears could play there, be safe, and get food. [Vision] So, they should all leave the drifting ice and safely swim to land. [Call to action]

Keep in mind that everyone who is affected by your leadership will want to know the same thing: "How will the changes impact me?" So, when you are crafting your communication points, be sure to be able to explain (1) how the changes will affect them, and (2) how the changes enable them to be more successful and feel better themselves.

Great communication pivots off an organizing concept, headline, mantra, and central message.

For example, *"We're going to be 1 or 2 or we're going to get out"* was one of Jack Welch's early organizing concepts at GE.

Or, *"A car in every driveway"* was the overarching message Ford deployed early in the 20th century.

The purpose of an organizing concept and overarching message is to anchor all your communication. A good place to find it is in your vision of the future, the call to action. Or it could be your overall guiding principle.

Writing about Jean Claude Brizard - Rochester, New York's new school superintendent at the time - Meaghan McDermott said,

His message for Rochester is that we must "make education personal."

> *"I read somewhere once that every child is a work of art,"* he said.

> *"Our task is to help create a masterpiece out of each. We need to get teachers and principals to a place where they can track the progress of each student and create the proper enrichment and intervention for each."*

He said he wants to create an environment in the district where if he asks a school principal about a specific student and their dreams, aspirations, struggles and achievement, he and school leaders will be able to have a meaningful dialogue about that child's future.[42]

Amplifiers

Amplifiers include the people that will help you drive your message and the media you leverage. There are always others influencing the people you want to influence. Think through stakeholders internally and externally through your eco-system all around the people you want to influence

---

[42] Meaghan M. McDermott, "Brizard takes city school district's reins today," Rochester Democrat and Chronicle, January 2, 2008. (Brizard has since moved on to head up Chicago's schools.)

---

including their bosses, peers, subordinates, mentors, advisors and the like. Find, nurture and deploy like-thinking allies in your quest.

The media you select are the methods or vehicles you choose to deliver your message. It is more common to distribute your message through multiple media. The options have exploded in quantity and kind, each one with slightly different effects on how the message is perceived. What people often fail to consider is that the same medium will have different effects on different people with different messages.

There is great opportunity here, and great danger. The same message sent via a press release will be perceived differently than the exact same message sent via Twitter, Instagram, WhatsApp or Facebook. A creative or fun free-for-all with a listserv can be great for some communication efforts—a friendly rivalry—and disastrous for others— like communicating a change in organizational structure. It's worth slowing down and thinking through the message, the media, and your objectives carefully.

Media will either be two-way, alternating, or one-way.

Two-Way Media

When it really matters, when the personal stakes are high, when you need to deploy words, tone, and body language to their fullest potential, and to soak in the other's words, tone, and body language you need two-way media. First prize is face-to-face, one-on-one, in the same space, live.

The ease and seeming intimacy of certain new media like e-mail and texts can lead to fateful errors of judgment about not using face-to-face, one-on-one communication when it should be used. A recent campaign for smart phones spoofs on such errors when a woman breaks up with her romantic partner by texting him while he sits across the table from her. Almost no one ever regrets lifting their fingers off the keyboard, getting out of their office and walking over, driving over, or flying over to have a face-to-face, one-on-one conversation. Choosing this correctly is a matter of leadership.

Small group meetings are particularly useful for pulling together diverse people to solve problems, explore issues, and have multiplayer conversations. Medium and large-group meetings and events are useful for disseminating knowledge and answering some questions live.

Videoconferences and video chat can communicate words, tone, and some body language without traveling. And phone is good for two-way communication of words and tone (but no body language.)

Alternating Media

These are one-way media that allow for almost instantaneous response. Indeed, they are so fast that they often feel like simultaneous two-way media. These include things like online chat, text messages and all sorts of new media being invented as you read. Use them. But don't mistake them for true two-way media.

One-Way Media

Platforms, mass and social media are useful for exchanging information and ideas without physical or temporal barriers. Mass, asynchronous communication enables 1) on-demand updates, 2) input from everyone across geographies, time zones, levels and cultures and 3) people to contribute their best thinking when they do their best thinking instead of when it's most convenient for you.

Why Audiences Get the Performances They Deserve[43]

Audiences get the performances they deserve. Those paying less attention get less attentive performers. Those listening quietly allow performers to do what they set out to do. Those that engage in the highest quality listening and appreciation inspire the highest quality performances and develop the highest quality relationships.

At an early moment in the most recent HATCH event, singer/songwriter Paul Durham gave an impassioned plea to the assembled group:

"As a musician, I'd like to ask for quiet during musicians' performances. We should treat musicians with at least the same respect with which we treat speakers – maybe even more, since the musicians are pouring their hearts and souls into their music."

And sure enough, later that evening we saw exactly what he was talking about when a handful of musicians came together to deliver an epic music set that reached into the audience's hearts and souls and made people break out into goose bumps, chills, tears and ongoing standing ovations.

---

[43] From George Bradt's November 5, 2015 Forbes.com article, "Why Audiences Get the Performance They Deserve"

The worst scenario is not listening at all. Then there are three levels of listening.

Level One Listening – Multi-tasking

Level one is listening while doing something else at the same time. Think about musicians in a bar or café. As Durham told me, *"When people are talking to each other while I'm playing, I'm really just providing background music."* The energy and passion performers put into providing background music is all that is required to produce the minimum viable product. They will comply with what they must do, but no more.

Level Two Listening – Attentive

Level two listening is what Durham asked for. The audience is quiet and open to receive the performer's message. Durham told me, *"When the audience is quiet, I can bring them up and down and back."* Essentially, attentive listening gives performers the space they need to do their thing. They will do their best to contribute to the experience.

Level Three Listening – Active and Interactive

Level three listening is active and interactive. Audience members go beyond receiving the performer's message to actively engaging with the performer and not only being open to being moved, but letting the performer know how they are feeling along the way. Think of the difference between a stand-up comic working with a silent audience and an audience feeding off the comic's performance and feeding it right back.

On the last evening of this event, we watched a transformation in Daniel Blue in the middle of one song. He started out great. The audience reacted. Then he took the performance to a whole new level. As he put it, *"Sometimes Duendé just takes over."* Duendé, as master storyteller Nick Bantock describes is *"the creative force flowing from the source and through the artist or storyteller."* An interactive audience actively assists that flow.

That's why audiences get the performances they deserve. Multi-task and you'll get the minimum viable performance. Listen attentively and you'll get the best a performer has to offer. Listen actively and you'll unleash the power of *Duendé* and help performers go to new levels.

Implications for Other Interactions

You've already figured out that this goes beyond performers. It's true of any conversation with any storyteller in any situation – personal or professional.

Multi-task while your child, spouse, friend, colleague, boss or subordinate is talking and you'll get the background music you deserve – until they get fed up and find a better audience.

Listen attentively and those communicating with you will give the conversation the best they've got.

Active listening is about being open to being moved and showing how you feel along the way. It's not about inserting your point of view. Be open, show your emotions and you'll unleash the power of *Duende* to take the conversation and the relationship to a whole new level.

If the relationships don't matter, go ahead and multi-task or cut people out of conversations in the name of efficiency, time management or other priorities. But for the relationships that do matter, investing in active listening is the best use of your time.

Perseverance

Manage your communication plan as an iterative set of concurrent conversations around a set of topics that you propose and guide. Shape it as best you can, but know that in most cases some element of your communication network will always be taking on a direction of its own, including ones you didn't anticipate or possibly may not like.

Be acutely aware of how different media get different results. If you really aren't interested in people airing their opinions about the newly announced merger, don't invite it. If you feel that you have a culture that can embrace this and can convert it to a positive energy-building activity, then you might want to consider it.

Sandy Rogers et al suggest loyalty is built on empathy, responsibility and generosity. [44] Empathetically make human connections, listening to learn.

---

[44] "Fierce Loyalty", Sandy Rogers, Shawn Moon, Leena Rinne, Amacom, October 2018

Lead with others' needs, taking responsibility for getting the real job done and following up to strengthen relationships while generously enabling, sharing and surprising others with unexpected extras.

You're going to need to be, do and say your message over and over again at different times, with different people, in different ways.

The Red Cross's Charley Shimanski[45]

Charley Shimanski's words inspire. His actions inspire. And they hold together because he firmly believes the importance of what he says and does. He exemplifies how new leaders can – and should – develop and implement organizing concepts which inspire others to embrace and execute their missions. To put it simply, Be. Do. Say.

George had the opportunity to spend some time with Charley at his first Red Cross Disaster Response Directors Conference. Charley had recently moved from being CEO of the Red Cross's Denver chapter to heading up the organization's overall disaster response. This was his onboarding coming out party with his top 180 or so leaders. He knew that what he communicated and how he communicated it would be critical. But he wasn't worried about it.

The reason he wasn't worried was that the Red Cross's mission is core to his being. George asked Charley what was most important to him. He didn't hesitate:

> *"Our people. They are not only the most important asset we have, they are what makes the American Red Cross what it is. They represent that segment of society that is willing to roll up its sleeves to help someone that that they've never met before."*

Charley went on to describe his thought process and organizing in preparing for the conference:

---

[45] From George Bradt's March 9, 2011 Forbes.com article, "How the Red Cross's Charley Shimanski Inspires Others with Communication at the Heart of the Mission"

"I start by getting a sense of what I want them to feel when they're done hearing from me — what I want them to feel, not hear me say....I wanted them to feel that they are at the core of what we do, that our success is on their shoulders. I wanted them to feel proud."

He reinforced his sense of pride in the Red Cross on a continual basis throughout the conference, talking about how the organization is often *"the best part of someone's worst day,"* and punctuating others' success stories with *"How cool is that? You should feel that that's pretty cool. I hope you do."*

He also shared his own stories, describing how he first volunteered for disaster response 25 years ago when he saw a local TV news broadcast on a boy lost in the Colorado mountains and just showed up and helped.

Charley went on to discuss how he spent 25 years as a member of Colorado's Alpine Rescue Team and a stint as president of the national Mountain Rescue Association — he mentioned how much the Red Cross has meant to him at very specific times in his life, particularly as a recipient of help from the Red Cross when he volunteered as a first-responder:

"There's no better cup of coffee than the cup of coffee served in a cardboard cup with a Red Cross on it because it's a cup of love."

Charley physically and emotionally puts his arms around people and draws them close to him, making them feel better about themselves. He does this face-to-face, one-on-one, and with his equally inspiring boss, Red Cross president and CEO Gail McGovern. Both of them reinforce the notion that disaster response is at *"the heart of the Red Cross's mission."* He reinforces this message continually in large groups, interviews and through his Twitter account — warning people of risks, cajoling them to help and complimenting good work.

Charley tells the story of people in a restaurant who hear the sound of a significant car accident. As he describes it,

- Many will go to the window to see what happened.
- Some will go to the curb to see what happens next.
- But a small number of those patrons will rush to the accident scene to be what happens next — helping out however they can to the best of their abilities.

Charley and the people he inspires through his communications are those who want to be what happens next. Be. Do. Say.

Everything Communicates

Not surprisingly, since we live in the midst of a communication revolution, the guidelines for communicating are changing dramatically. As much as we would like to treat communication as a logical, sequential, ongoing communication campaign, in many cases, it's more essential to manage it as an iterative set of concurrent conversations:

- Take into account the network of multiple stakeholders as you specifically identify your target audiences.

- Discover and leverage your core organizing concept as the foundation for guiding iterative concurrent conversations by seeding and reinforcing communication points through a wide variety of media with no compromises on trustworthiness and authenticity.

- Monitor and adjust as appropriate on an ongoing basis.

Don't hesitate to deploy an old school logical, sequential communication campaign when appropriate – though we expect that to be the case less and less over time.

Charley inspires – as should you.

Communicating at a Point of Inflection[46]

The most effective communication is outcome-focused in a contextually appropriate way. Think about what matters and why to you and to the people you're trying to influence. Then think about the best approach to moving those people in the right direction. Bring it all to fruition with personalized communication pushing for the right level of engagement delivered by situationally appropriate leaders in the right manner.

Deloitte's change strategy leader, Mike Bentley took me through the communication aspects of their new change management methodology. The core of it is focusing on the desired outcome, driving the right balance of will and skill across four types of transformation (Tech Slam, Process Acceleration, Modernization, or True Transformation,) leveraging three enablers (Affinity, style, and commitment.)

---

[46] From George Bradt's September 12, 2018 Forbes.com article, "Communicating at a Point of Inflection"

Desired Outcome

Bentley started his explanation where all change initiatives should start – the desired outcome. As Bentley told me "Organizations fail because they're missing what they're really trying to do." He went on to explain that what leaders really care about is how to drive success and "How to structure the right approach to get to that success."

Will and Skill

The right approach to change management builds people's willingness to change and ability to deliver what is required during and after the change. The balance of those two is different across the four types of transformations. Bentley took me through them:

Four Transformation Types

1. *Tech Slam* – Very Information Technology (IT) focused. Most transformation programs have a huge IT component. A pure Tech Slam is about replacing a technology platform. Generally, these involve no organizational changes. The key is building the required skills for employees to be able to use the new systems. Thus, these involve heavy investment in training and processes and procedures with less investment in motivation. These programs can be effective with their limited scope

2. *Process Acceleration* – These are about adjusting and evolving defined processes to increase efficiency or speed. There may be some job role changes. Similar to Tech Slams, these are focused on increasing ability by building skills in existing people and adding new people.

3. *Modernization* – These involve changing technology and updating people. They also involve changes to operations. Some organizations use this as a response to digital changes. People generally understand they have to change the technology and process to do things like letting customers place orders on line. There's a bias to building skills and some need to motivate people to be willing to change. This means leaders need to explain why the change is happening and the strategy behind it to get people to buy into the change and think differently.

4. *True Transformation* is at the other end of spectrum. These are the most disruptive transformations at points of inflection. The aim is to change the way things are done. These require rewiring organizations, redefining cultures, leadership, and organizational operating models. While there's certainly a skill or ability-building component, the key is the willingness component.

Three Enablers

Bentley suggests looking at three enablers in improving people's willingness to change.

1. *Affinity* is the first enabler. Messaging is most effective when it comes from the group to which people are most closely affiliated. For example a finance person might affiliate with the geographic team they are part of , the business unit or the overall finance function, suggesting different communication leaders.

2. *Style.* Transformational communication should nest within organizations operational styles. Not all styles work in all organizations. For example, command and control communication won't work in organizations with more bias to supporting each other, sharing responsibilities or working with guided accountability.

3. *Commitment.* Understand the level of engagement you need. Bentley calls this commitment versus support. It's a different way of looking at compliance vs. contribution vs. commitment. Bentley suggests that a True Transformation cannot be successful without at least 15% of people crossing the tipping point to commit to the program.

Business Presenting 101

Sandy Linver built a whole expertise on presenting and communicating and shared it with people all around the world through her Speakeasy organization. This section relies heavily on that. Most of the ideas are hers, with some adaptation.

Her basic framework is that presenting is about bridging gaps. Start by figuring out what the impact on your audience needs to be. Then figure out where they are now. Then move them to where they need to be. The steps are:

1. Identify your destination.[47] Choose the influence and impact you will have on your audience. Be specific about what you want them to be aware of, understand, believe, feel, and do (learn, contribute, decide, say, act.)

2. Be explicit about unstated Xs. There's also a hidden X. Think through how you want your audience to think and feel about you.

---

[47] Much of this is based on work by Sandy Linver and her company Speakeasy, also laid out in her book Speak and get Results, Simon and Schuster 1994

3. Assess current reality. Figure out where your audience is now and how they got there. What are they aware of, understand, believe about their situation and about you? Which aspects of that help? Which get in the way? Consider potential obstacles, negative rumors, hecklers or other sabotage, legal requirements, and unintended consequences of what you say or do. Think about hidden influencers. Consider scenarios.

4. Reevaluate destination in light of assumptions about audience. Now go back and relook at your destination (and hidden Xs.) Given what you just laid out about the current reality, can you still get all the way to the target you set in step 1? Or do you need to get there in steps?

5. Bridge the gap with your organizing concept, message and communication points. This is key – choosing what to communicate to bridge the gap between the current reality/platform for change and your destination vision. Think through what people need to be aware of, understand (rationally,) believe and feel (emotionally) to answer the call to action and move from the current reality to that destination. This spawns your organizing concept (strategy) and message (words.)

Your organizing concept/message sets up questions, likely including

1. Why anyone should listen to you? Why should they care?

2. What should they be aware of, understand, believe, feel? What they should do next: learn, contribute, decide, say, act?

3. How should they move forward?

These are closely related to Ethos, Pathos and Logos. Ethos gets at the intentions and competence of the speaker and their empathy with the audience. (Me.) Pathos is about the feelings the speaker engenders in the audience (You.) Logos is about evidence and facts that will win the audience over, leading them to action. (Us.)

Ideally, you'll communicate emotionally, rationally and inspirationally:

- Emotionally, establishing an emotional connection with your audience (Ethos)

- Rationally, laying out the brutal facts of the current reality as a platform for change (Logos)

- Inspirationally, pointing the way to a vision of a better future with a call to action. (Pathos)

These form the heart of your communication, pulling in the right personal stories to establish your intentions and competence, the right illustrations to connect with the audience, and the right evidence, facts and clear next steps to compel them to action. ("Right" means necessary and sufficient.)

Craft your message based on what people need to be aware of, understand, believe, and feel to move from current reality to the desired destination.

> Platform for change:
>
> Vision of a better future:
>
> Call to action:
>
> => Organizing Concept/Message headline
>
> Three main message or support points

6. Prepare your opening. To frame and capture their attention. Note default option for "presenting" to senior executives should probably be a one page/one slide executive summary that frames the conversation and makes all your main points. A good format for that (and the basic flow of your presentation) is:

1. Headline message (Lede) (i.e. "Seeking your agreement to buy X")

2. Situation/problem/platform for change (nut) (Company X is siphoning off customers)

3. Desired impact/solution/vision of a better future (Buy, merge, protect our base, and grow)

4. Plan/next steps/call to action (Offer $XXB all-cash. Specific steps.)

7. Prepare your closing. To cement your message, knowing that people remember what they see first and last more than what comes in the middle.

8. Deliver the message. Deliver emotionally, rationally and inspirationally in line with your plan.

Implement with the best vehicles in the optimum combination with the best timing. Get clear on who and what influences whom. This is where you pull in your amplifiers. And don't forget to plan out how you can best plant the follow-up seeds.

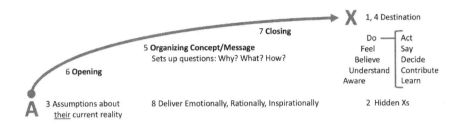

1. **Choose your destination.**[48] Impact on audience: aware of, understand, believe, feel, and do (learn, contribute, decide, say, act.)

2. **Be explicit about unstated Xs.** How audience should think and feel about you. (Hidden X)

3. **Assess current reality.** Where audience is now. Obstacles. Rumors. Influencers.

4. **Reevaluate destination** in light of assumptions about audience. Required steps?

5. **Bridge the gap with your organizing concept/message**

   Think through what people need to be aware of, understand (rationally,) believe, and feel (emotionally) to answer the call to action and move from the current reality to that destination. Plus three questions to serve as framework for presentation.

6. **Prepare opening.** To capture their attention. (For senior executives should probably have a one page/one slide executive summary that makes all your main points.)

7. **Prepare closing.** To cement your message, knowing that people remember what they see first and last more than what comes in the middle.

8. **Deliver the communication.** Emotionally. Rationally. Inspirationally.

To customize this document, download Tool 4.1 from the BRAVE Leadership page on www.onboardingtools.com.

---

[48] Much of this is based on work by Speakeasy's Sandy Linver, also laid out in her book Speak and get Results, Simon and Schuster 1994

Press Interviews

If you concentrate on answering the interviewer's questions in a press interview, you're putting your result in their hands. If you're lucky, their agenda matches yours, leading to a happy result.

Don't do that.

Hoping for luck is not a plan.

Instead, concentrate on what you want to communicate and use the interviewer's questions as cues to help you do that. Now you're in charge. And you make the interviewer's job easier. Instead of piecing together a story, they can tell your story – with their perspective on it.

Net, take control of the interview. Time is on your side if you stay focused on what you want to communicate and you control the dialogue, just as it's on others' sides if they control the dialogue.

George has done a lot of interviews through the years. He continues to be interviewed by others and to interview leaders for his articles for Forbes and other publications. He will not go into an interview until he is clear on the "slant" of the article if he's doing the interview or the three points he wants to make if he's being interviewed. And he's generally transparent about his going-in point of view on the story. He's found it to be helpful because very few people look at interviews as win-lose propositions. Instead, they want to collaborate to craft a story valuable for the audience.

In many ways, interviews are moments of impact. Like all moments of impact, think through the prelude, manage the moment, and follow-up.

Prepare

> **Objective**—Be clear on the single objective for the interview. What do you want the outcome and impact to be?

> **Anticipate questions**—Know the interviewer, the audience, and their interest factors (competition, conflict, controversy, consequences, familiar person, heartstrings, humor, problem, progress, success, unknown, unusual, wants/needs.)

Twitter is a fantastic tool for this. Almost by definition, journalists want people to read what they write. So, many of them Tweet. It's astounding what you can learn about interviewers by reading their recent Tweets. In one case, George figured out that someone who was about to interview him was a rabid Philadelphia sports fan. So George chose Philadelphia sports examples to illustrate the points he made.

Approach—There are always different ways to get to your objective. Figure out the most appropriate approach for the interviewer and their audience. This will lead to:

Key communication points: Get clear on the key points you want to drive (three maximum.) This is the most important thing to do to allow you to do more than just answer questions (merely cues for your key points.) These points need:

Support: Facts, personal experience, contrast/compare, analogy, expert opinion, analysis, definition, statistics, and examples (similar to support for writing.)

Deliver

Be clear, concise, complete (do one thing well,) constructive, credible, controversial, captivating, correct (must correct significant errors on the part of interviewer or press.)

Be yourself, liked, prepared, enthusiastic, specific, anecdotal, a listener, a bridge, cool.

Follow Through

Deliver on commitments you make to the interviewer. If you say you're going to send them more information, send it. Soon.

Think through what worked particularly well and less well to improve for the future.

Tool 4.4
Press Interview Management

Prepare

Objective—What do you want out of the interaction?

Anticipate questions—Know interviewer, audience, and their interest factors (competition, conflict, controversy, consequences, familiar person, heartstrings, humor, problem, progress, success, unknown, unusual, wants/needs.)

Approach—What way do you choose to go about achieving the objective? There are always different ways to get there. Consider them and choose one. This will lead to:

Key communication points: Key points you want to drive (three maximum.) This will allow you to do more than just answer questions. (merely cues for your key points.) These points need:

Support: Facts, personal experience, contrast/compare, analogy, expert opinion, analysis, definition, statistics, and examples.

Deliver

Be clear, concise, complete (do one thing well,) constructive, credible, controversial, captivating, correct (must correct significant errors on the part of interviewer or press.)

Be yourself, liked, prepared, enthusiastic, specific, anecdotal, a listener, a bridge, cool.

Follow Through

Deliver on commitments.

Think through what worked particularly well and less well to improve for the future.

Emotional, Rational, Inspirational Communication

There are a number of shorthand ways to think about your communication. People have used Ethos (me), Pathos (you), Logos (us) for centuries. The Stockdale Paradox's combination of confronting the brutal facts and faith in the future works well in dire circumstances.

Points of inflection are going to be jarring for some. You won't be able to identify all the people that are going to be emotionally impacted in advance. You won't go very far wrong by communicating emotionally, rationally and inspirationally with everyone.

Emotional

Connect with your audience by being authentic, relatable, vulnerable and compassionate as you empathize with how the crisis is affecting them personally – Mayfield and Mayfield's empathetic language.[49] This is the marriage of Ethos (me) and Pathos (you.) As one of our partners used to say, "No one cares how much you know until they know how much you care."

Rational

Lay out the hard facts of the current situation – in detail with a calm, composed, polite and authoritative tone and manner. This is the first part of the Stockdale Paradox. We're defining facts here as things that any rational person would agree are true no matter what bias or perspective they bring to the situation – objective, scientific truths as opposed to subjective, personal, cultural or political truths, opinions or conclusions.

Inspirational

Inspire others by thinking ahead, painting an optimistic view of a future they care about, and calling people to practical actions they can take to be part of the solution - instilling confidence in themselves with Mayfield and Mayfield's meaning-making and direction-giving language.

The optimistic future view goes to meaning and purpose: mission, vision and values. Ground all your communication in values: be – do – say.

The call to practical action is direction-giving, making people part of the solution.

---

[49] Jacqueline and Milton Mayfield, *Leader Communication Strategies - Critical Paths to Improving Employee Commitment* – American Business Review, June 2002

BRAVE People Leadership

The most effective leaders lead three concurrent processes for their organizations and boards - strategic, operational and organizational (as well as paying attention to governance and culture.) You can apply the BRAVE leadership framework to the organizational process – people leadership.

Environment - Where to play? (Context)

Begin with where to play. Do this with Future Capability Planning (Tool 4.5) to create a picture of what your organization must look like to implement your strategy and evolve your culture over time. Look at both individuals and the future organizational structure: generalists, specialists, hierarchy, matrix, decentralization, or portfolio. This creates gaps with your current reality. Think through the various ways to fill those gaps including:

- Developing current people by evolving their attitudes and building knowledge, skills, and experience on top of their existing talents.
- Acquiring new people with required attitude, talents and differential perspectives soon, then building their knowledge, skills and experience.
- Acquiring new people with the required attitude, talent, knowledge, skills, experience and perspectives just in time as needed.

Values - What matters and why? (Purpose)

These are exactly the same as your overall organization's mission, vision and guiding principles. They always apply.

Attitudes - How to win? (Choices)

To be ADEPT, an organization must acquire, develop, encourage, plan and transition its people. The question to answer here is what's required for your organization to win versus its competitors. Some organizations, like Coca-Cola in the 1990s, win by over-investing in acquiring superior talent. Others, like Procter & Gamble in the 1980s, win by over-investing in developing its existing talent. Still others meet their objectives by encouraging their people with superior compensation, benefits or atmosphere.

Relationships - How to connect? (Communication)

Connect with different people differently depending upon who they are, how much they care and what you need from them in terms of engagement:

- Other than those dead set on detracting, people will generally **comply** if they are aware of what they need to do. This can be accomplished with indirect communication.
- Getting people to **contribute** requires understanding. If they know what is needed, they can deliver. If they understand why it is needed, they may find different ways to do even more than asked. This requires direct communication so they can ask questions.
- **Commitment** is a whole different game. People don't commit to leaders, teams or organizations. They commit to causes, to doing good for others. This involves going well beyond understanding to belief. Getting there requires connecting at an emotional level with those who care most.

Behaviors - What impact? (Implementation)

Experienced leaders' #1 regret looking back on their careers is not moving fast enough on people. Figure out who is outstanding, effective and ineffective as well as who is in the right role and treat them accordingly, acquiring, developing and encouraging in line with your priorities.

	Ineffective	Effective	Outstanding
Right Role	Invest	Support	Cherish
Wrong Role	Move out	Move laterally	Promote

This is all about building ADEPT teams by Acquiring, Developing, Planning and Transitioning people.

Acquire

There are several steps to acquiring the right people in the right way: scope roles and align all around that scope, recruiting brief and onboarding plan, identify prospects, recruit and select, attract and onboard them so they can deliver better results faster.

Develop

Talent development should flow from your talent reviews. This is about assessing performance drivers and using a 70/20/10 approach to building experience, skills and knowledge required for people to deliver in current and future roles (70% on the job; 20% interactions with others; 10% formal learning events.) Unlike future capability and succession planning which start with the desired future state and work backwards, this starts with the current reality and builds off that.

Encourage

Encourage with direction, resources, authority to make tactical decisions within strategic bounds, and accountability, leading to engaged people. But "Employee engagement" is too blunt a measure. You need to distinguish between compliant, contributing and committed people and your prompts.

Plan

Future capability planning, succession planning and contingency planning are each critical. Embed all three in your organizational processes so you're ready for the future and ready to react to unexpected changes.

- As described above, **Future Capability Planning** is the primary link between your strategic process and organizational process. Use it to create a gap between your future organizational needs and current reality and a plan to fill those gaps.
- Succession Planning gives you a picture of the people that can take the place of current leaders when they move on – their "successors."
- Contingency Planning gives you a picture of how you're going to fill the gap when a leader needs to be replaced unexpectedly. Think like football coach Bill Belichick and always have a "Next man up, ready to go, no excuses."[50]

Transition

While there are some people moves that you must make quickly at a point of inflection, generally you can evolve people into new roles over time. Not all transitions are up. Some are across. Some are down. And some are out.

Across: Some people need to move to different roles at the same level to broaden their knowledge or skills or because their existing strengths can make a bigger impact somewhere else.

Down: Some people may want to move down to roles with less scope, responsibility, or stress as they move into different life stages: adding kids, spouse retiring, and so on.

Out: Some people are in the wrong role. They may never have been the right person for the role or the role may have changed around them. Either way, when it's time for them to go do something different, it's time.

---

[50] Per George Bradt's January 9, 2018 Forbes article on "Lessons in Leadership…"

Deciding to move someone out of a role is a big decision not to be taken lightly. It can be painful – for them and for you. Remember also that the number one thing experienced leaders regret is not moving fast enough on people. And remember that the number one thing high performers want is for someone to get the low performers out of their way. So, think the moves through thoroughly. Then act decisively at points of inflection.

Leadership is about inspiring, enabling and empowering others to do their absolute best, together, to realize a meaningful and rewarding shared purpose. If things stayed constant, people wouldn't have to transition to new roles. Everything is constantly changing, so transitioning people to new roles is often a big part of inspiring, enabling and empowering them to do their absolute best.

While you'll be cycling through ADEPT on a continual basis, make sure you've got a future capability plan in place to guide your efforts.

Tool 4.5
Future Capability Planning

Strategic priorities:

Future organization, culture, capabilities and perspectives required by those priorities:

Existing organization, culture, capabilities and perspectives:

Gaps:

Current people to develop/plan to develop them to fill those gaps:

People to recruit early on and develop/plan to develop them:

People to recruit later:

Plans to fill other gaps:

How to Hire Great People

Adding the right people to your team in the right way is one of the most important aspects of leading through a point of inflection. A good first step is crafting a complete recruiting and onboarding plan and timeline. Then get important players aligned around your plan. Think in terms of:

Define – Develop – Prepare – Source – Recruit – Interview – Assess

Define

The most effective and successful searches start with a proper definition of the role. Everyone on the team should be aligned around:

- What matters and why to us as an organization?
- Why are we filling this particular role? Talent gap? Backfill? Other?
- New hire's responsibilities? Tasks? Interdependencies and reporting? Expectations? Key performance Indicators?
- Required/nice to have strengths: talents, knowledge and skills?
- Employee value proposition for the new hire:

  Good for others
  - THE WORK ITSELF: Impact on others, sense of personal achievement (Social consciousness)

  Good at it
  - THE OPPORTUNITY: Leverage and build my strengths - stability, development, training and development

  Good for me
  - TANGIBLE REWARDS: Salary, Bonus, Long Term Incentive; Benefits - health, dental, retirement, tuition, disability, paid time off and life insurance.
  - THE ORGANIZATION: Positive work environment, and a healthy work-life balance (Workplace flexibility)
  - PEOPLE: Company culture/affiliation: Positive relationships and team spirit with colleagues and managers.

A critical step in preparation is getting everyone on the same page regarding what you're look for. That page is the Recruiting Brief laying out position, mission and responsibilities, picture of success, strengths, motivation, and fit considerations.

Tool 4.6
RECRUITING BRIEF

Recruit for: Job Title, Department, Compensation Grade, Start Date

Mission/responsibilities:

Why position exists	
Objectives/goals/outcomes	
Impact on the rest of the organization	
Specific responsibilities	
Organizational relationships & interdependencies	

Vision (picture of success)

Strengths

Talents	
Knowledge (education, training, qualifications)	
Skills (technical, interpersonal, business)	
Relevant experience	

Motivation

How activities fit with person's likes/dislikes/ideal job criteria	
How to progress towards long-term goal	

Fit

Values	
Work style, characteristics - Company's	
Work style, characteristics - Group's	
Work style, characteristics Supervisor's	

Copyright© PrimeGenesis®. To customize this document, download Tool 4.6 from the BRAVE Leadership page on www.onboardingtools.com.

You may delegate the detailed work around developing, preparing, sourcing and recruiting candidates to others. In any case, you'll want to interview the final candidates for your most important positions yourself. When you do, make your first question, "Why would you want this job?"

Why Your First Interview Question Should Be "Why Would You Want This Job?"[51]

Start job interviews by asking candidates why they would want the job. It's the most important of the only three interview questions so you want the cleanest answer to it. Then, their answer to that first question will inform other questions you ask – if any. Their answer will let you know whether their bias is to do good for others, things they are good at, or good for themselves. Note we're talking about "buying" interviews, not "selling" recruiting or sourcing calls.

Recall the only three interview questions are 1) Will you love the job? 2) Can you do the job? and 3) Can we tolerate working with you? Or strengths, motivation and fit. Every question you've ever asked, ever been asked, or ever will ask is a sub-set of one of those three. The strengths assessment is relatively straightforward – they either have the strengths required or they do not. The fit question is tricky as you're trying to line up their personal preferences across behaviors, relationships, attitudes, values and the environment with your culture. That leaves motivation as the most important thing to get at in an interview.

Recall also that happiness is good. Actually, it's three goods: doing good for others, doing things you're good at, and doing good for yourself. Everyone operates with some balance of the three – with different biases and balances. The answer to the motivation question, "Why would you want this job?" reveals that bias:

- If they talk about the impact and effect they could have on others, their bias is most likely to do good for others.

---

[51] From George Bradt's January 2, 2019 Forbes.com article, "Why Your First Interview Question Should Be "Why Would You Want This Job?"

- If they talk about how the job could allow them to leverage their strengths, their bias is most likely to do things they are good at.
- If they talk about how the job could fit with their own goals or progresses them towards those goals, their bias is most likely to do things that are good for them.

Knowing that bias informs where you should go with the interview. Essentially,

- If their bias fits with what you're looking for, go on to probe strengths and fit.
- If you're not sure, dig deeper into their motivations, by going through different levels of why or impact questions until you are sure.
- If their bias does not fit with what you're looking for, end the interview. How you do this can range from going through the motions of completing the interview, to letting them ask you questions, to walking out.

Order matters. Everything you do and say biases what follows. If you start your interview by probing strengths and then ask someone why they would want the job, they may try to mold their answer to fit what they infer is important to you from your questions about strengths. They may think your question is another way for you to get at strengths. Similarly, if you start your interview by probing fit and then ask about motivation, they may try to mold their question to convince you of their fit. So, start with the motivation question – without any biases.

While the world generally needs more other focused leaders, this may not be true for your particular situation. The strongest leaders and strongest organizations over time will, indeed be other-focused. They think outside-in, starting with the good they can do for others. They are the leaders and organizations people will want to work for over time, will want to learn from, and will want to help.

Still, you may need to focus more on strengths, building required strengths to ensure your near-term survival so you can be other focused later. You may need to be a little more self-focused so you can attract and leverage people who think "good for me" first, so you can build some momentum.

The choice is yours. In any case, figuring out what drives the person you're interviewing is your most important task in an interview. Make it your first task.

Managing People Who are Doing Well – and Not So Well

You have to develop both the strong and the less strong.

Develop (Recall this as the "D" in ADEPT People Management)

Identify the most important drivers of performance, assess individuals against them and then develop their skills and knowledge in those areas to be more successful in their current role and prepare them for future roles.

Gallup suggests that a strength is a combination of talent, skill, and knowledge. Since talent is innate, you can't do anything to build that. So your focus should be on skills and knowledge. We also agree with Gallup that your focus should be on helping people get even stronger in areas of strength rather than trying to develop their weaknesses into strengths. That process will be frustrating for everyone involved. It is far better to build on their strengths, and help them mitigate their weaknesses in other ways.[52]

> *Talent:* Innate, naturally occurring preferences.
> *Knowledge:* Acquired through learning.
> *Skills:* Acquired through practice.
> *Experience* Acquired through activities, projects, programs, roles.

Development Plans

Development plans are all about helping people develop. The trap is that some managers focus development plans exclusively on fixing problems. As noted above, we think it's better to help people further develop their strengths (as well as fixing some problems.)

In that light are the following ten steps:

1. Select the areas for development.
2. Lay out a developmental objective for the period (generally one year.)
3. Work out a developmental approach and plan.
4. Be explicit about the resources to be deployed including money, personnel, and time.
5. Clarify the responsibilities of person being developed.
6. Agree on the responsibilities of the manager/coach – generally you.
7. Agree on timing and the milestones along the way.
8. Implement.
9. Monitor and track.
10. Adjust as appropriate.

---

[52] Buckingham and Clifton, Now Discover Your Strengths, Free Press 2001.

Strengths to develop:

Developmental goal for the period – build on innate talent with learned knowledge, practiced skill, relevant experience

Developmental approach/plan – reading, courses training to learn knowledge; on-the-job or other to practice skills; discrete activities, projects, programs, assignments or roles to gain relevant experience:

Resources to be deployed – managers, coaches, trainers:

Responsibilities of person being developed:

Responsibilities of manager/coach:

Milestones/timing:

Encourage (Recall this as the "E" in ADEPT People Management)

Whoever taught you to say "please" and "thank you" was prescient. This is the key to encouraging people on your team.

"Please" is all about clarity around expectations: objectives, goals, and measures. It's about enabling people to succeed by making sure they have the direction, resources, tools, and support they need and then getting out of their way. (And getting others out of their way.)

"Thank you" is about providing the recognition and rewards that encourage each individual. Multiple studies have shown that, in general, people are positively motivated by things like the type of work they are doing, challenge and achievement, promotion prospects, responsibility, and recognition or esteem. Things like salary, relationship with colleagues, working conditions, and their supervisor's style are basic factors that don't motivate if they are in the acceptable range, but can quickly demotivate if there is a problem.

So, the general prescription isn't all that hard. Make sure the basic factors are good enough and won't cause problems, and invest in the real motivators. It is not about motivating people. It is about enabling people to succeed so they can tap into their own inner motivations. Seek to enable your team.

You can encourage people by:

Clarifying how their individual roles fit with the broader group.

Establishing individual SMARTER goals for them.

Goal Setting

John Michael Loh, United States Air Force Air Combat Command during the first Gulf War said: "*I used to believe that if it doesn't get measured, it doesn't get done. Now I say if it doesn't get measured it doesn't get approved . . . you need to manage by facts, not gut feel.*"

George Doran created an acronym for thinking about goals: SMART[53] - Specific, Measurable, Actionable/Attainable, Relevant, Time bound. Others added Encouraging and Rewarded to make them SMARTER. In brief, goals work when they are:
- Specific – Concrete objectives are easier to achieve and track.
- Measurable – If you can't measure it, you can't manage it.
- Actionable/Attainable – Things we can make happen or influence (and achieve.)
- Relevant – To our overall mission, strategy, plan.
- Time bound – Including milestones along the way
- Encouraging/Exciting – To the people involved.
- Rewarded – When they are accomplished.

If an eight-year-old can't tell if the goal was achieved or not at the end of the period, it's not SMARTER enough.

---

[53] Doran, G. T. (1981.) There's a S.M.A.R.T. way to write management's goals and objectives. Management Review, Volume 70, Issue 11(AMA FORUM,) pp. 35–36

SMARTER: Specific, Measurable, Actionable/Attainable, Relevant, Time bound, Encouraging, Rewarded

- Specific – Concrete objectives are easier to achieve and track.
- Measurable – If you can't measure it, you can't manage it.
- Actionable/Attainable – Things we can make happen or influence (and achieve.)
- Relevant – To our overall mission, strategy, plan
- Time bound – Including milestones along the way.
- Encouraging/Exciting – To the people involved.
- Rewarded – When they are accomplished.

To customize this document, download Tool 4.16 from the BRAVE Leadership page on www.onboardingtools.com.

Team Charter

Goals work for individuals and teams. For project-focused teams, it's also useful to give them a charter. This should include:

Description/Scope - a brief summary of the project's what and why (objectives/goals, context) and potentially key interdependencies and guidelines so others can see quickly how this project fits with others.

Objectives/Goals - Clarify what specific, measurable results (SMARTER) they are asked to deliver.

Context - Provide the information that led to the objectives/goals you gave them. A part of this is the intent behind the objectives so they know how their output will impact others and what will happen after the objective is achieved.

Resources - Explain the human, financial, and operational resources available to the team. Also make them aware of other teams, groups, units working in parallel, supporting or interdependent areas.

Guidelines - Clarify what the team can and cannot do with regard to roles and decisions. Lay out the interdependencies between the team being chartered and the other teams involved.

Accountability - Be clear on accountability structure, update timing, completion timing.

TEAM CHARTER

Useful for getting teams off to the best start.

Description/Scope: Overall summary

Write this last - a brief summary of the work's what and why (objectives/goals, context) and potentially key interdependencies and guidelines, so all can see quickly how this work fits with others' work.

Objectives/Goals/Desired Result: WHAT

Charge the team with delivering SMARTER results - Specific, Measurable, Achievable, Realistic, Time-Bound, Encouraging, Rewarded. Start by making it clear what you expect the team to get done:

- Specific – Concrete objectives are easier to achieve and track.
- Measurable – If you can't measure it, you can't manage it.
- Actionable/Attainable – Things they can make happen or influence (and achieve).
- Relevant – To our overall mission, strategy, plan
- Time bound – Including milestones along the way.
- Encouraging/Exciting – To the people involved.
- Rewarded – When they are accomplished.

Context and Intent: WHY

Share the information that led to objectives/goals in terms of the organization's overall purpose, objective, strategies, positioning, values, as well as how this work fits within that and helps move things in that direction.

- Provide any insights you have into customers, collaborators, capabilities, conditions or competitors.
- Get at the expected level of complication (number of parts) and complexity (predictability of parts' interactions) of the project, expected risks and ways to mitigate those risks.
- Discuss the intent behind the objectives. Explain why this matters to your customers, colleagues, you, the team – key benefits.
- Lay out what's going to happen after objective is achieved, how will others use the team's output.

Resources: HOW

Lay out the human, financial, technical, and operational resources available. Note other teams, groups, units working in parallel, supporting or interdependent areas. Help the team understand the resources they have available and whom they can, should and must work with. This may or may not include a steering committee, executive sponsor/champion, program or project leader, program or project manager assisting that leader, project management or transformation office helping coordinate across teams.

Authority/Guidelines: HOW

Clarify what the team can and cannot do with regard to roles and decisions. In particular, be clear on what things the team can decide on its own, and what things the team must recommend to its approving authority. Lay out the interdependencies between the team being chartered and the other teams involved. Be clear on the difference between policies (that they must adhere to,) guidelines (that they should adhere to unless they have a good reason not to do so,) and mindset (that should underpin all.)

Accountability - HOW KNOW

Be clear on accountability structure (RACI: Accountable, Responsible, Consulted, Informed,) update timing, completion timing. This is about **how you're going to track and measure success.** In general, tasks get managed/tracked daily, projects weekly, programs monthly, and strategic priorities quarterly.

- **Approving Authority:** Passes accountability on to someone else, retaining approval/decision rights.
- **Accountable:** Overall ownership of results. Drives decisions. Ensures implementation.
- **Responsible:** Does defined work (and signs off on their portion of the work.)
- **Consulted:** Provides input. (Could be advice or concurrence) - Two-way conversation.
- **Informed:** Kept up-to-date - One-way communication.
- **Support** - Assist in completing the work.

Required Resources

Just as it is important for people to understand how their goals fit with the rest of the organization, it is equally important to make sure that people have the resources and support (internally and externally) they need to achieve their goals. It would be silly to ask the sales force to sell 100 widgets per day with plant manufacturing capacity of 50 per day. You would end up with unhappy customers, furious salespeople, and nervous breakdowns throughout the plant.

To help reinforce the creation, deployment, and achievement of goals, you need assistance. That assistance comes in the form of knowledge, skills, experience, tools, resources, guidelines, linking performance and consequences, and driving actions and milestones along the way.

1. **Knowledge:** This boils down to facts that you are aware of. The greater your breadth and depth, the better.

2. **Skills:** These are the how-to's or capabilities. Know what those skills are, and know which ones you have to practice to develop.

3. **Experience** gained from relevantly similar activities, projects, programs, assignments or roles.

4. **Tools:** Without the right equipment, you cannot reach your goals. You must know what equipment is needed, what you have, and how to fill the gap.

5. **Resources:** The three key resource needs are human, financial, and operational. Make sure that resources are available to support your established goals in each of these areas. If not, you either have to change your goals to make them more realistic, or increase your access to the needed resource.

6. **Guidelines:** Establish boundaries so that everyone knows how far they can run. Everyone should know the things that you cannot do because they are outside the clearly established guidelines.

7. **Link between performance and consequences:** Make the link between performance and consequences explicit. If that link is properly established, everyone should know how the results will be rated. As many organizations get larger and more bureaucratic, they tend to bunch people's annual raises in a narrow range, doing things like giving those who meet expectations a 3 percent to 5 percent raise and those who exceed a 4 percent to 6 percent raise. Over time, this has a devastating effect on performance because

people see that they are not going to be rewarded for putting in extra effort to over deliver and won't get punished for marginal under delivery.

8. **Actions and milestones along the way:** You cannot do midcourse corrections if you do not know where you're supposed to be at midcourse. It is far easier to spot a problem when someone says, "we produced 9 widgets last month versus a goal of 30" than when someone says, "we experienced normal start up issues but remain fully committed to producing 360 widgets this year."

Team Captain[54]

Having the right team ingredients is not enough until a leader inspires, enables and empowers the individuals to do their absolute best together as a team. Having the right coach, players, money and strategy are necessary, but not sufficient until you have such a leader. The implication for you is to ensure there is a "captain class" BRAVE leader in some role on each of your most important teams, and then prompt and encourage them to do what they need to do.

In researching his brilliant book, *The Captain Class,* Sam Walker identified and analyzed 16 freakishly successful sports teams and another 100+ that were almost as successful over the past century. The common driver on the most successful teams from Cuba women's volleyball to All Blacks rugby to French handball to the NY Yankees was not coach, stars, money or strategy but the presence of a courageous, dogged, passionate, aggressive leader. In every case, the team's extraordinary run started when the captain joined the team and ended when the captain left.

Walker looked at professional teams that had five or more members who interacted with opponents, competed together (unlike gymnastics or skiing,) played a "major" sport against the world's top competition with sufficient opportunity to prove themselves, dominated for at least four years with records that stand alone.

---

[54] From George Bradt's July 11, 2017 Forbes.com article, "Why the Key to a High Performing Team is the Captain Class BRAVE Leader"

These teams had stars like Pele (Brazil,) DiMaggio (Yankees) and Messi (Barcelona) who often delivered at moments of truth. While these stars got the glory or the girl (including Marilyn Monroe,) they were too me-focused to lead others to extraordinary heights. It was the less skilled, less flashy team captains like Bellini (Brazil,) Berra (Yankees) and Payol (Barcelona) who inspired, enabled and empowered others to perform at their best together through their own obsession with the whole team's collective success.

Walker highlights several attributes these captain leaders had in common that conveniently line up with the BRAVE leadership framework. The art of the general (or CEO) is arranging forces before the battle at a strategic level, starting with the question of where to play. The art of the captain is leading forces in battle tactically, dealing with questions of what matters and why, how to win, how to connect and what impact. Walker's attributes line up with these.

Values – What matters and why

Strong convictions and **courage** to stand apart and stand up for the team to anyone (starting with the conviction of the importance of the team over everything else including self).

Attitudes – How win

Extreme **doggedness** and focus in competition almost to the point of madness – like playing through concussions (All Blacks' Buck Shelford,) broken toes (USA soccer's Carla Overbeck) or even a heart attack (USSR hockey's Valeri Vasiliev).

Ironclad emotional control - including having a "kill switch" to turn off distracting thoughts - like French handball's Jerome Fernandez' father's imminent death.

Relationships – How to connect

Motivates others with **passionate** nonverbal displays - like the Pittsburgh Steelers Jack Lambert's letting the blood from his hand gash smear his jersey and pants.

A low-key, practical, and democratic communication style – with a bias to private words of encouragement or correction over public speeches.

<u>Behaviors – What impact</u>

Aggressive play up to and often beyond the limits of the rules – including taking penalties when they lead to better results for the team - like Cuba Volleyball's Mireya Luis taking trash talking to new heights against Brazil.

A willingness to do thankless jobs in the shadows of more acclaimed teammates – like carrying water or bags or cleaning up or accepting less than market value in pay to create space versus a team salary cap to bring in other players the way the Spurs' Tim Duncan did.

Implications

- Teams need stars and leaders. Don't confuse the two. Make sure you have the star designer, builder, salesperson, logistical expert or the like on the team. AND ensure there is a captain class BRAVE leader.
- Prompt them to lead – from any chair. Their title, level or formal designation is irrelevant.
- Get out of the way to let them do what they do.
- Encourage them with positive reinforcement appropriate for them.

People Management

The basic concept here is that on the spot feedback can save you all sorts of time and angst over the long term and earn you respect. Tool 4.22 is George's cheat sheet to a couple of useful techniques.

The overriding idea is to notice and react to events. When you notice something. start by clarifying what happened and why. Confirm what you think you saw. Then make a choice. If this is something you need to change, drop into criticizing or managing differences mode. If this is something you want to encourage, drop into crediting or building mode.

Constructive criticism

If you choose to criticize, it's generally best to itemize the merits (things you value) and concerns. Discuss these with the person involved, trying to find a way to retain the merits and eliminate the concerns.

> *"Suzi, love your blouse. Not sure the really short cut off jeans go best with it here. Perhaps you can find something else that will go even better with it at work."*

Managing differences

This happens when the person you're trying to influence sees things totally differently than you do. The prescription here is to explore the differences. Try to zero in on what's really important. Then find ways to alter the restrictions. Explore some alternatives. If you can't agree, end the conversation.

"But I love my cut offs."

"They look great. Just not in the office."

"But I love them."

"Could you wear them to and from the office and change into something different while you're here?"

"That would be a hassle."

"Okay then. I'm going to outvote you. No more cut offs in the office."

Credit

This is the fun stuff. Any time you can pat someone on the back is a good time – providing it's real. People see through gratuitous praise. This simple formula forces you to think through what and why you're crediting for and makes it real to the person being praised.

1. Make a general reference to the area you're crediting. *"Nice job with that new customer yesterday."*
2. Make a specific reference to what the individual did. *"The way you established rapport by referencing your shared interest in Wallyball was wonderful."*
3. Note the personal qualities that helped the person do what they did. *"It's another example of how your thoroughness in preparing for meetings pays off."*
4. Close with the resulting benefits to the organization and person. *"By the way, your work was a huge contributor to us closing the sale this morning. You're getting the commission."*

Building

Building is another good news communication – if done right. This is one that can go very wrong very quickly.

Start by acknowledging the connection to the original idea. *"Love your idea about a team lunch tomorrow to help us bond."*

Add value by modifying, adding benefits, bringing in other applications, or coming up with new ways to realize the original intent. *"We could invite some of our allies as well."*

The risk is in changing the idea in a way that destroys the original intent. *"Instead of a lunch, perhaps you can all come to my office at the end of the day to see the slides from my recent trip to WallaWalla."*

Finally, check back with the idea owner to make sure you've preserved their idea. (Back to inviting allies.) *"Do you think the addition of allies would be a good thing or would it dilute the core team's bonding?"*

Tool 4.18
People Management Tools

Event: Clarify what, why. Then confirm; change by criticizing or managing differences; maintain by crediting and building.

Clarify and confirm – additional information about what and

Constructive criticism
1. Itemize merits and concerns
2. Discuss how to retain merits and eliminate concerns
3. Summarize

Managing differences
1. Explore difference – what's important? How to alter restrictions
2. Explore alternatives
3. End the conversation – It's okay to decide differently

Credit
1. General reference to area crediting
2. Specific reference to what individual did
3. Personal qualities that helped person do what they did
4. Resulting benefits to organization and person

Building
1. Acknowledge connection
2. Add value: modify, add benefits, other applications, new ways to realize original intent
3. Check back with idea owner to make sure you've preserved their idea

To customize this document, download Tool 4.18 from the BRAVE Leadership page on www.onboardingtools.com.

Managing Behavior

Sometime in the last century, George attended a workshop on managing behavior by Paul Brown. Brown's basic model has stuck with George and he's been using it ever since.

1. **Pinpoint** the specific behavior to be changed. Then ask yourself if it is legitimate to push the person to change. It is legitimate if the behavior is impacting either a) the individual's output, b) others' output, or c) the individual's future career.

2. **Track** occurrences of the behavior and decide if it's worth the effort to change it. If it happens once in a blue moon (a month in which there are two full moons) then don't worry. If it happens 31 times a day, that's a different story.

3. **Analyze** the ABCs: Antecedents, Behavior, Consequences and balance of consequences

4. **Change the environment** by either prompting new behavior (antecedent) or changing the balance of consequences so there are more negative and less positive consequences of undesired behavior and more positive and less negative consequences of desired behavior.

   It's stunning how often people get this wrong, actually providing positive consequences to undesired behavior – like re-starting meetings to accommodate people that are late. At other times, people provide negative consequences to desired behavior – like making people on time to meetings listen to the same things twice.

5. **Evaluate** by comparing the new behaviors to your baseline.

The key to this whole thing is changing the balance of consequences – and often reducing the positive consequences of undesired behavior.

Pinpoint   Specific behavior to be changed

Question whether it's legitimate to push the change:

Is it impacting the individual's output?

Is it impacting others' output?

Is it impacting the individual's future career?

Track   Quantify occurrences of behavior

Worth the effort to change?

Analyze Antecedents

Behavior

Consequences – balance of consequences

Change the environment

Antecedents

Consequences

Evaluate by comparing to baseline

To customize this document, download Tool 4.19 from the BRAVE Leadership page on www.onboardingtools.com.

Transformational change requires aligning plans, people and practices around a shared purpose. Tackling those pieces with the right approach and resources step-by-step in stages instead of all at once is often the difference between success and failure. Do four things:

1. Align plans, people and practices around a shared purpose.
2. Manage the transition in stages with different approaches and resources at each stage as appropriate.
3. Jettison each stage's excess baggage before it gets in the way of the next stage's success.
4. Celebrate your early successes.

Performance Assessment

It's highly useful to assess performance at the end of the period in order to make sure you keep doing what works and improve what needs to be improved.

Start with impact and influence. Impact is about results versus objectives – the what. If you've got SMARTER goals in place these should be self-evident. Influence is about how people got things done and fit with culture.

Then look at learnings and accomplishments: what worked? What need to improve? What learned about self?

Take a look at strengths and gaps and career interests (if you haven't put in place an up-to-date career plan.)

Use those to set new objectives.

Performance assessments are an excellent time to drive the overall business goals.

Gillian knew that excellent candidate follow-up made their recruiting business outperform their competitors. However, she had a challenge getting her team members to spend time on what they considered to be a menial task – that is, it didn't fit into the completion of finishing a mandate. Although she pushed how important it was, giving examples, it never really clicked.

Finally, she took the opportunity at each individual's mid-year review to explain how candidate management done correctly leads to new business, good candidates, and good word-of-mouth referrals, helping the overall state of the business. Conversely, by not conducting this task, they were losing out to their competitors.

Gillian saw the lights bulbs switch on immediately. Even though she had rattled on about this many times over in meetings, she had never tied it to how this small menial task affected the overall state of the business. Since then, she tries to explain the "Why?" in as much detail as possible. Now, once everyone understands how their roles impact the business, they buy in and energy increases.

Tool 4.20
Performance Assessment

Impact - Results versus objectives (What):

Influence - How (including 360° feedback as appropriate):

What worked/keep doing:

What needs to improve/stop/start doing:

What learned about self:

Strengths (Innate talent, learned knowledge, practices skills, relevant experience):

Gaps:

Career interests:

New objectives (mission-critical impact, culture adaptation/evolution):

Framework for Turning Individuals' Strengths into Team Synergies[55]

Employees perform at different levels, when on different teams, in different situations with different people. That probably makes sense to everyone. Why then do so few leaders spend so little time looking for synergies on their teams and so much time looking at individual performance? Because realizing synergies is hard work.

Phil and Allan Maymin and Eugene Shen began their "Skills Plus Minus" presentation at the MIT Sloan Sports Analytics Conference by asking who was basketball's better point guard from 2006 to 2008, Deron Williams (Utah Jazz) or Chris Paul (New Orleans Hornets).

The data is inconclusive with regard to the original question, but it does show that either player would have been even more valuable had he been on the other team. Had the Jazz and the Hornets done a one-for-one, straight up trade, each team would have been better off. Their stars might or might not have performed better, but the entire teams would have.

The presenters looked at things like offensive and defensive ball handling, rebounding and scoring. Then they looked at the same things in the company of other players to determine the positive and negative impact of players on each other. If two players each steal the ball from their opponents two times per game on their own, but together steal the ball five times per game when on the court together, that's a positive synergy.

Of course, it's important to understand the strengths of the individuals on your team. That always will be important. But that's just the first step. The only way to optimize synergies on a team is to leverage differentiated individual strengths in complementary ways.

In a hypothetical example, one manager is particularly strong at managing details, one at operations, and one is particularly strong at encouraging creativity. Unfortunately, the guy with the operating strength is managing the group that needs to be creative; the more creative guy is managing a group that needed to pay attention to details; and the detail-oriented manager is trying manage a complex operation. Moving each to the right role frees everyone up to perform better.

---

[55] From George Bradt's September 18, 2012 Forbes.com article, "Framework for Turning Individuals' Strengths into Team Synergies"

It's not just about the individuals. It's about the individuals in the context of the tasks that need to get done and the other individuals involved.

Let us propose five steps flowing from the BRAVE leadership framework:
1. Understand the context: where to play and what matters.
2. Determine the attitude, relationships and behaviors required.
3. Evaluate attitudinal, relationship and behavioral strengths.
4. Structure work so individuals complement each other's strengths.
5. Monitor, evaluate and adjust along the way.

The pivot point is leveraging complementary strengths across attitudinal, relationship and behavioral elements. The specifics of those are going to be different in each different situation. That gets us back to the initial point. But now you've got a framework. So there's no excuse not to pay as much attention to potential team synergies as you do to individuals' strengths.

Implications for you: Think team, not collection of individuals.

Partnerships

This chapter has been mostly about leading followers. Often you have to lead peers. One of the trickiest questions is how to beat the odds and make equal peer partnerships work.[56]

Most of the time, equal partnerships are hard to make work because they are not actually equal. Furthermore, even if they are equal for one brief shining moment, they don't stay equal. If you want to beat the odds and make your partnership work, you either need to have a shared interest, a shared framework for making decisions, or the leverage required to influence your partners to do the right things the right way (your way.)

"Partnership: A relationship usually involving close cooperation between parties having specified and joint rights and responsibilities." – Merriam Webster's 3rd definition

Arguably the most critical "specified" rights are decision rights – who makes what decisions. In unequal partnerships in which it's clear who's making which decisions, decision-making generally works. Conversely, equal partners, trying to make all decisions jointly, are generally doomed to failure. Eventually they disagree, get frustrated, and grow apart. The answer to how to make it work is right there in the definition: be specifically and explicitly clear who's making which decisions and how.

---

[56] From George Bradt's December 15, 2020 Forbes article on "*How to Beat the Odds and Make Equal Partnerships Work.*"

Many of George's books (including this one) have been co-authored. Things worked well when one person was the lead author and made the final decisions. Alternately, things worked well when we gave different authors specific responsibilities for specific sections so they could focus on those sections, become experts, and make decisions for "their" sections.

Conversely, it was more challenging when decisions were shared and we had to come to consensus. It's hard to get everyone to agree - especially without an agreed framework for decision making. True for books, businesses, and almost any situation where two or more people have to cooperate with each other. Which gets us right back to shared interest, frameworks and leverage.

Shared Interest

First prize is for partners to share the same context, objectives, and values. Having those in place makes it much easier for you to cooperate and share rights and responsibilities. And having those in place provides a platform for constructive conflict. If your interests are truly shared, you can't help but looking out for each other's best interests at all times. You all can assume positive intent and view differences as arising from complementary strengths.

Trouble arises when situational changes effect different partners differently. These can be changes in their personal situation like marriage, children, or changes in other businesses or occupations. These can be changes in the business situation across customers, collaborators, associates, competitors, or external conditions. Any of these have the ability to change the relative importance of the partnership to the different partners.

Shared Frameworks

As noted in an earlier article, frameworks are the basic conceptual structures that people use to flesh out their ideas. They help people know where to start, and they focus and guide thinking about how to achieve purpose. If you and your partners agree on frameworks for decision-making, it makes it easier for you and everyone you are working with to make decisions. All know what information to look at, what precedents apply and how different people will approach decisions.

Leverage

Leverage is about altering the balance of consequences – often by making unseen consequences visible. The essence of a balance of consequence is the comparison of positive and negative repercussions of making different choices.

Even if your partner can make a decision without you, and even if your partner follows a different decision-making framework, you can still influence that decision by applying leverage.

Remember the marshmallow test? A child is given a marshmallow or pretzel and told they can eat it if they want, but if they wait fifteen minutes, they can have two. The incremental treat is leverage.

Your leverage with your partners is going to range from positive to negative, from small to large, from indirect to direct, and from immediate to deferred. In general, make sure you are:

- Applying positive leverage to reinforce desired choices and actions versus undesired,

- Applying small leverage in doses over time or large leverage when needed urgently,

- Helping others understand the impact of your indirect leverage.

- Helping others understand the short-term versus long-term tradeoffs inherent in your deferred leverage.

Not all partnerships work. Even when they do work, they may not work forever. As you find yourself moving from shared interest to shared frameworks to leverage, be on the lookout for the moment when it's time to stop partnering at all.

Summary: How to Connect

Everything you do or don't say, do, listen to and observe communicates and drives how you connect – 24/7, forever. Own and leverage a single, simplifying message in ongoing iterative conversations. Instilling the right feelings by who you are, what you do and what you say (Be. Do. Say.)

- MAP your communication with your message, amplifiers, and perseverance.
- When onboarding yourself, get a head start, manage the message, set direction and build the team and sustain momentum and evolve.
- Build an ADEPT team, by acquiring, developing, encouraging, planning and transitioning talent.
- Evolve your organization in line with your strategic changes, moving from generalists to specialists to a hierarchy, decentralization, matrix as appropriate. **

5 *Behaviors:* Getting Things Done

Environment, values, attitude and relationships all inform behaviors and what impact you and your team make. Ultimately, you lead with your feet, with what you do, more than with what you say. So, focus everything and everyone on those few behaviors with the greatest impact through your point of inflection.

Depending upon which part of the value chain you're focused on, different behaviors will have greater impacts. Note all organizations do all of these. The most effective leaders vary their leadership approach by situation, keeping an overall main focus while adjusting for specific instances.

- **Design** - If your organizational focus is design, your main job as a leader is to *enable* your designers and inventors with freeing support.

- **Produce** - If your focus is production, don't be afraid to command and control things to *enforce* your polices to create stability.

- **Deliver or distribute** – Delivering or distributing is about linkages. *Enroll* people across the matrix to accept shared responsibility.

- **Service** - If your focus is service, make sure everyone in your organization is committed to the customer as boss and is prepared to react and respond as required by that boss. Be the chief *experience* officer, guiding close to the customer decentralized accountability.

- **Sell** - Everybody has to sell and market. As Drucker says, the purpose of business is to create customers.

Delegating, Innovating, and Negotiating

Learning to delegate is a non-optional exercise. The core of leadership is inspiring, enabling and empowering others. This means giving them things to do that you could theoretically do yourself.

Delegating[57]

Scope is a function of resources and time. If the scope of what you're trying to accomplish is too much to get done in a high-quality way in the time allotted, you have to add resources, add time, or cut back the scope. In other words, say "no" to some of the less important items and non-value-adding steps. Think in terms of your options for completing tasks:

1. Do well yourself
2. Do yourself, but just well enough
3. Delegate and supervise
4. Delegate and trust
5. Do later
6. Do never

Working harder is often counter-productive. As Simpler Consulting CEO Marc Hafer explained to George, the world is full of heroes who get in the way – the "*bright, passionate, compassionate ones who are blinded by their passion.*" They strive to "*get it done*" at any cost, not realizing the true cost is the diminished effort against other, higher value adding activities. With that in mind, more on your options:

Do well yourself

These are the things your end customer values most. Say no and downplay, delegate, cut back, and avoid other things so you can spend more time to do your absolute best on these critical activities. The more people you have in your organization, the less of these you should have. CEOs for example should really have only one or maybe two strategically important things they're trying to do well themselves.

---

[57] Adapted from George Bradt's Forbes.com articles: November 29, 2012: "Work Less, Create More Value - The Art of Delegating" and June 25, 2019: "The Time Management Flip – Enable Others Before Doing Your Own Work"

Do yourself, but just well enough

Accept the need to do these things yourself. But they are not as important as some others. So, do them and do them well enough to satisfy the stakeholders who need them to fit into what they are doing for the end customer – and no better.

Delegate and supervise

The items you delegate and supervise are important. You want them done well, but there isn't enough value in doing them yourself. Or perhaps, there are others who can do the work better than you. Either way, you care about these items enough to supervise the work. This is the realm of managers and supervisors, tactically shifting resources throughout the implementation of priority programs and projects.

Delegate and trust

Delegating and trusting is about giving someone else clear **direction**, the **resources** they need, the **authority** to make tactical choices within the strategic bounds you've set and **accountability** for their results. This is real empowerment. It works only if you have confidence in your lieutenants. If you don't have that, replace them with those deserving confidence.

Do later

Things you decide to do later choices are temporary reprieves for the important but not urgent. Team members can refocus their time, though not all their attention because they want to be ready for "later." "Do later" projects aren't bad ideas. They're just not priorities now.

Do never

Choosing not to do something ever is a permanent time saver. Team members can focus all their time and attention on more important things, banishing the "something else" from their minds forever. Some of these are bad ideas. My partner Harry Kangis suggests that choosing not to pursue bad ideas is easy. The hard choice is choosing not to do something that's a good idea – for someone else.

The Time Management Flip and Directed Delegation

Think leverage, not efficiency. Make the Time Management Flip to flip the order. Do things to enable others to do "their" work before you do "your" work. Make the strategic choices, creating and allocating resources. Give them clear direction, accountability, boundaries, and authority. Then, get out of the way. "Your" work will contract over time as you delegate and trust more.

The next time a task arises, ask yourself about the end value and then determine the best approach. Then go one step further to utilize directed delegation for tasks you are delegating. Direct work to the people with the most applicable strengths and aligned interests and provide those people with clear direction in realizing the vision and values in order to deliver better results for all.

- **Direction**. Clarify objectives and goals and provide context so they understand your motivation (why,) rationale and intent.
- **Resources**. Provide appropriate resources.
- **Authority**. Give them the authority they need to make tactical decisions with clear guidelines to what they can/cannot do.
- **Accountability**. Clarify accountability structure and timing.

When people see or hear "leader", they generally think of interpersonal leaders inspiring, enabling and empowering teams. While those interpersonal leaders are of critical import, the world needs artistic leaders and scientific leaders just as much. And you need to play your part. Webster defines leader as "a person who rules, guides, or inspires others."

Artistic leaders inspire by influencing feelings. They help us take new approaches to how we see, hear, taste, smell and touch things. You can find these leaders creating new designs, new art, and the like. These people generally have no interest in ruling or guiding. They are all about changing perceptions.

Scientific leaders guide and inspire by influencing knowledge with their thinking and ideas. You can find them creating new technologies, doing research and writing, teaching and the like. Their ideas tend to be well thought-through, supported by data and analysis, and logical. These people develop structure and frameworks that help others solve problems.

Interpersonal leaders can be found ruling, guiding and inspiring at the head of their interpersonal cohort whether it's a team, organization, or political entity. They come in all shapes and sizes, and influence actions in different ways. The common dimension across interpersonal leaders is that they are leading other people.

Net, artistic leaders inspire by influencing feelings. Scientific leaders guide and inspire by influencing knowledge. Interpersonal leaders rule, guide and inspire to influence actions. And, oh by the way, these are not mutual exclusive. Leaders can lead in more than one way. Keep this in mind as you're deciding to whom to delegate which tasks.

Innovating

In general, you should delegate as much as you can to allow you to focus as much of your energy on your team and on innovating. If you don't understand the importance of team building go back and re-read chapter 4. Regarding innovating, you can apply the BRAVE framework:

Environment - Where to play? (Context)

Start with a shared understanding of your organization's innovation needs. Webster defines innovation as "the introduction of something new." Linda Hill suggests it should be useful as well. Doug Hall[58] says it needs to be "meaningfully unique," meaning someone will pay more for it.

Be clear on you need something new verses introducing existing inventions to your organization, market or the world. Think through the challenge you face. Do you seek revolutionary, disruptive, "LEAP" innovation or merely evolutionary, incremental, sustaining core innovation?

Values - What matters and why? (Purpose)

Reconfirm your organization's mission, vision and guiding principles to guide everything else you do.

---

[58] Per George Bradt's November 13, 2018 Forbes.com article, "How to Lead the Change from Haphazard to Systematic Innovation"

Attitudes - How to win? (Choices)

Aim your efforts at business concepts and models and not just product and service inventions and improvements. There's more value in strategic innovation across the entire value chain than in one-off efforts. Look across products, processes, services, technologies and business models. Make sure you're leading in a way that inspires, enables and empowers innovation.

Relationships - How to connect? (Communication)

As Linda Hill says, you must "unleash the talents and passions of the many from the stranglehold of the few." Sid Lee's Will Travis talks about the value of giving people permission to explore "in the friction zone" with problems to solve, watching them play, accumulating and collaborating to create and strengthen insights, and rewarding small wins to build momentum.

Look at jobs to be done, domains, and innovation architecture. Manage constraints while moving from idea to business concept. Doug Hall insists on the importance of new stimuli to prompt new thinking and, as Skarzynski and Crosswhite suggest:

"Don't start with new ideas. Start with new insights, which help you develop new and different perspectives about your particular innovation challenge."

Behaviors - What impact? (Implementation)

Innovation is inherently messy. Bring some order to the chaos with a define – discover/create – develop/iterate - assess – deliver/implement and scale approach combining IDEO's Human-Centered Design, BAC's Scratch and Doug Hall's Innovation Engineering System approaches:

Define

- Define what you're looking for and then use Hall's Blue Cards to charter teams. These lay out your purpose, what you see as the "very important" opportunity or system improvement, clarity on whether you're looking for "LEAP" or "core" innovation on a long-term strategic or project-specific basis, whether this applies to the entire organization or a specific division or department, your name for the effort, a narrative describing how you got here, the strategic mission, strategic exclusions (barriers,) tactical constraints (like design, time, resources, investment, regulation,) areas for project exploration or long-term innovation.

Discover/Create

- Prepare by learning, listening, observing patterns of behavior, points of pain and inconvenience to gain insights across five dimensions: 1) Customer insights, 2) Market discontinuities, 3) Competencies and strategic assets, 4) Industry orthodoxies, 5) Seeing and mapping white space.
- Generate ideas - with champions to carry them through and the right level of innovation for each initiative: 1) Acquisitions (like Ebay acquiring PayPal,) 2) Sister companies (like Amazon keeping Zappos in the family but separate,) 3) Separate divisions (like Disney's Imagineering or Procter & Gamble's Miami Valley Labs,) 4) Skunk works (like Lockheed's Skunk Works,) 5) Giving all specific amounts of time to innovate (like 3M and Google do,) 6) Special circumstances (like Hack-a-thons at Facebook and others,) 7) Not for us (like Dom Perignon.)
- Use Hall's Yellow Cards to capture idea headlines, customer/stakeholder, problem, promise, proof, price/cost, raw math, death threats (to the idea,) passion (why we care.) They clarify whether the idea addresses a LEAP or Core opportunity or system in line with the Blue Card used to charter the group.
- This is the time for what Linda Hill calls "Creative Abrasion" or collaborative problem-solving to co-create ideas.
- Develop minimum viable products/rapid prototypes.

Develop/Iterate

- Get responses from different users, peers, others.
- Modify and test again with what Hill calls "Creative Agility" or discovery-driven learning/testing.
- Make sure to iterate your process as well in Plan – Do – Study – Act cycles.

Analyze

- Analyze, filter and decipher those responses as part of what Hill calls "Creative Resolution" or integrated decision-making and then

Deliver/implement and scale across products, processes, services, technologies and business models through your point of inflection.

A key part of your implementation will be locking in on the innovation positioning so all understand:

- o Customer and problem (think target)
- o Customer promise (think benefit)
- o Product/Service/System proof (think reason to believe)
- o Meaningfully unique (dramatic difference)

Where to play - MIT's Neri Oxman – The Beginner's Mind

Neri Oxman suggests the beginner's mind is filled with innocence. "*As child you think you are shrinking when you see an airplane take off.*" Oxman and her Mediated Matters group at the MIT Media Lab have moved beyond "*bio mimicry*" to actually designing with nature in pursuit of bio-inspired fabrication. She told George about their new silk pavilion, actually created by 6500 silk worms. She envisions scaling this idea with a swarm of 3-D printers to expand beyond any one printer's gantry as part of her search for "*variations in kind*" moving well beyond "*better, faster, cheaper, bigger.*"

In an interview at the C2 Conference in Montreal, Oxman told George about her "*fork in the road.*" She's a trained architect and designer. The choice she faced was whether to focus on design or go into research. She chose research because it gave her the opportunity to design her own technology. It allowed her to influence both products and processes – both influenced by nature.

She's a big proponent of variations in kind – true innovations. She's convinced these come from "being vulnerable", not so much from solving a problem as from innocence and different worldview. It's that different worldview that allows the innovator to come up with new to the world solutions when problems do come.

Focus on solving someone's problem – Bobbi Brown

Bobbi Brown was on a TV shoot and had forgotten her eyeliner. To make do, she grabbed a Q-Tip and used it to brush some mascara on her eyelids, solving her immediate problem. The next morning, she was surprised to see the mascara still in place. The gel in the mascara had made it last. She called her design team and had them mock up the first gel liner – now her most copied product. Many of Brown's innovations have come from thinking "*It would make so much sense if…*" She describes these as "*random ideas mixed with common sense.*"

This was just one of the examples Brown shared with George. She also related how using a clean baby wipe to remove her makeup prompted her to create a baby-wipe-like makeup remover. And she told George about wanting to wear cowboy boots with jeans she had. When they wouldn't fit, she cut them off – the boots, not the jeans. These stories all go to her philosophy of having a clear vision, but then being open to change direction as needed. She's good at this because she seems to be able to understand what's needed next. Definitely a big idea to change direction before anyone else knows you need to.

George admits this was a difficult interview for him. He's still not sure he understands what the difference is between mascara and eyeliner. But Brown made it easy for George. She seemed to genuinely enjoy teaching a complete ignoramus (George) about what she did. George thinks that's part of what enables her to innovate and connect.

Follow Through: Diane Von Furstenberg

Diane von Furstenberg is clear that her wrap dress happened "*by accident.*" Her original T-shirts morphed into wrap tops and then into wrap dresses. They caught on and have stayed in fashion for almost 40 years because they are "*easy, proper, decent, and flattering and sexy.*" They may have happened by accident originally, but their ongoing success is directly related to von Furstenberg's drive to succeed on her own (at first,) prove she was not a one-shot wonder (later,) and leave a strong brand as her legacy (now.)

It's often difficult to separate the brand from the personality. On the one hand, while a major attribute of the Virgin brand is Richard Branson, and a major attribute of Apple was Steve Jobs, and a major attribute of Walmart was Sam Walton, in each of these cases the brand name and the personality are different. Those brands will survive their founders. It's harder when the founder's name and brand name match as they do with Diane von Furstenberg.

Of course, there are examples of success. The Disney brand is thriving – perhaps because its sub-brands are anything but Mickey Mouse. McDonald's is a golden arch, and maybe a clown. Very very few people think of Richard and Maurice.

Von Furstenberg has spent time thinking about the difference between the brand and herself. A big part of her follow through is setting up the brand as her legacy: celebrating freedom, empowering women, color, print, bold, effortless, sexy, on the go. Of course, she's a living example of the brand now. Over time, others need to step up as that example.

Why Adding Constraints Increases Innovation[59]

It is counterintuitive. You would think the more scope, time and resources you have, the easier it would be to innovate. Chris Denson, Director, Ignition Factory at Omnicom Media Group says you would be wrong. He suggests "The more limited you are, the more creative you have to be. Time constraints eliminate second guesses. Constraint is a unifier." This may explain why larger resource-rich organizations struggle with revolutionary innovation.

Let's look at Denson's points one by one.

Mission constraint is a unifier.

HATCH's Yarrow Kraner describes the constraints adventure hostel Selina's cofounder Rafi Museri has had to deal with "to reimagine a new vertical, catering to a quickly evolving digital nomad audience, this group needed to move quickly, efficiently, and responsibly to scale at a pace that would put them on the map quickly, without breaking the bank. All of the furniture and fixtures are hand-crafted by up-cycling found trash, rubble, and debris and giving second life to previously consumed resources.

To accomplish scaling at this rate with such artisan craftsmanship, Selina's Creative Director Oz Zechovoy has been training ex-gang members to be carpenters, builders, and welders. They are quickly growing from three locations currently to 10 by the end of 2016, and over 90 locations within the next 4 years, creating hundreds of new jobs and positively impacting Panama's economy."

In this case, the constraint forcing innovation is the overlapping missions: to build adventure hostels catering to the evolving digital nomad audience *and*, at the same time, to give products and people in Panama a second chance.

---

[59] From George Bradt's March 9, 2016 Forbes.com article, "Why Adding Constraints Increases Innovation"

Time constraints eliminate second guesses.

An example of time constraints forcing innovation is found in the way NASA team members came together during the Apollo 13 crisis. Right from *"Houston, we've had a problem,"* the team reacted flexibly and fluidly to a dramatic and unwelcome new reality—a crippling explosion en route, in space.

The team went beyond its standard operating procedures and what its equipment was "designed to do" to exploring what it "could do." Through tight, on-the-fly collaboration, the team did in minutes what normally took hours, in hours what normally took days, and in days what normally took months. This innovation was critical to getting the crew home safely.

The constraint here was all about time. Not only was failure not an option, but success had to come fast. Very fast. This imperative broke down all sorts of petty barriers and got everyone rallied around what really mattered, leading to innovation out of necessity.

The more resource limited you are, the more creative you have to be.

Kraner describes Kalu Yala is an example of just this: the world's most sustainable community - that started as a conscious real estate play, but the founder realized that it would take millions of dollars to build out a destination before attracting buyers, and flipped into an institution as it's first priority, teaching while learning about sustainable best practices.

Can civilization and nature coexist? Can our diverse cultures coexist with each other?

The first phase, and the foundation of the plan is the Institute; an educational platform for students from around the world who are collecting, implementing, and documenting best practices in sustainable living. The work-study program has hosted students from all over the world from 25 countries and 150 colleges.

Kalu Yala's Jimmy Stice didn't set out to build an institute. But, as he put it, "Constraints are what give a design its focus and ultimately, its true shape."

Implications

Innovation requires one of the only three types of creativity: connective, component or blank page. The surprise is that these thrive on less resources rather than more. Don't over-water your plants and don't over-resource your innovation:

- Narrow and focus the mission.
- Give tight deadlines.
- Limit resources.

If you need innovation, put people in a box with limited resources and a tight deadline. The real innovators will thrive on the challenge and find surprising, new and perhaps revolutionary ways out of the box.

Why the Route to Creativity Runs Through Distress[60]

Want to prompt creativity? Make someone unhappy. If people are happy, there's no need to change. But if people are faced with others' or their own distress, they will work to find creative ways to bridge the gap from bad to good and unhappiness to happiness.

Happiness is good - three goods: good for others, good at it, good for me. This means there are three opportunities to create distress: others' distress, strengths mismatch or personal distress.

Others' Distress

Many of society's advances were born out of someone's finding new, creative ways to solve others' problems.

Fire was born out of the need for a better way to keep warm.

Vaccinations were born out of the need to protect people from diseases.

---

[60] From George Bradt's April 19, 2017 Forbes.com article, "Why the Route to Creativity Runs Through Distress"

Pet Rocks were born out of the existential need for more meaningful holiday gifts.

The list goes on and on.

Einstein told us that we couldn't solve problems with the same level of thinking that created them. When some people's level of distress with others' unhappiness reaches a breaking point, they move to new levels of thinking and create new ways to solve the underlying problems.

Prompt creativity by helping people see others' needs.

Distress from Strengths Mismatch

The world needs different types of leaders: artistic, scientific and interpersonal. Those leaders have different strengths and different ways of thinking. Some of the most creative ideas have come when those leaders are forced to think in different ways.

Doug Hall has been forcing people to do this for decades. Doug was trained as a chemical engineer and as a circus clown. He was a brand manager at Procter & Gamble, eventually becoming "Master Marketing Inventor" there before starting his company, Eureka Ranch. In its early days, Eureka Ranch drove *"creativity, stimulus and fun"* and helped all sorts of business executives play outside of their comfort zone by deploying things like Nerf guns, water cannons and whoopee cushions.

Howard Gardner suggests there are nine different types of intelligence:

1. Naturalist Intelligence (Nature Smart)
2. Musical Intelligence
3. Logical-Mathematical Intelligence (Number/Reasoning Smart)
4. Existential Intelligence (Getting at the meaning of life)
5. Interpersonal Intelligence (People Smart)
6. Bodily-Kinesthetic Intelligence
7. Linguistic Intelligence (Word Smart)
8. Intra-personal Intelligence (Self Smart)
9. Spatial Intelligence (Visual/picture Smart)

Thus, stimulate different leaders' creativity by getting them to access different types of intelligence than they normally do.

- Stimulate artistic leaders outside of their visual, kinesthetic, musical, linguistic comfort zones.
- Stimulate scientific leaders outside of their naturalistic, logical-mathematical, existential comfort zones. (Though I'm not sure anyone is ever really comfortable pondering the meaning of life.)
- Stimulate interpersonal outside of their intra-personal and interpersonal comfort zones, getting them to think like artistic or scientific leaders.

This all comes down to prompting creativity by making people think or act in new ways.

Personal Distress

Brand Communication agency Sid Lee's Will Travis will tell you that if the road to creativity runs through distress, the road to extreme creativity runs through extreme distress. Will has climbed several of the world's highest summits including Vinson Massif in Antarctica in the most brutal 45 degrees below zero Centigrade conditions imaginable, motor biked with The Paris Dakar and traversed the 18,000 Khardung La pass in the Himalayas and generally put himself in extremely stressful situations.

These experiences have helped Will both see things in different ways and keep things in perspective. As he put it,

Facing situations of life and death implications elevates ones vision way above the severity of the business landscape, resulting in both centered and humanistic decision making, that business school nor mentors can never teach.

Will uses this perspective to help the people he leads face and manage their own fears. It's painful when a client cold heartedly rejects a creative team's heart invested work. But we have to keep it in perspective that its' not a life-threatening situation. Will suggests

> *"You have to fail…Failure puts you in a friction zone, puts you in a zone where you have to make a decision, you have to change and do something different to survive and move on."*

SETTING THE STAGE FOR BRAVE INNOVATION

Environment - Where to play? (Context)

>The introduction of something new and useful

>Revolutionary/disruptive, evolutionary/incremental & sustaining

Values - What matters and why? (Purpose)

>In line with overall mission, vision, guiding principles

Attitudes - How to win? (Choices)

>Products, processes, services, technologies and business model

Relationships - How to connect? (Communication)

>"Unleash the talents and passions of the many from the stranglehold of the few" – co-create

Behaviors - What impact? (Implementation)

>Manage through the system:
>
>**DEFINE** *(Purpose – team charter)*
>
>**DISCOVER/CREATE** *(Creative abrasion/collaborative problem solving)* – leverage diverse strengths
>
>**DEVELOP/ITERATE** *(Creative agility/discovery-driven learning)* – "Current Best Thinking"
>
>**ASSESS** *(Creative resolution/integrated decision-making)* – drowning ugly ducklings
>
>**DELIVER/IMPLEMENT & SCALE**

Influencing[61]

Everyone balances doing good for others, doing things they are good at, and doing good for themselves. Other-focused leaders think first about how to do good for others while self-focused leaders begin with their own needs in mind. Thus, other-focused leaders instinctively do what Lee Miller suggests can help everyone improve their ability to influence others – begin with a "U Perspective."

U Perspective

The U Perspective is the core principle in Lee Miller and Barbara Jackson's book, *UP Influence, Power and the U Perspective - The Art of Getting What You Want.* At its base, U Perspective is about seeing things from the other's perspective. Miller explains how people can use that technique in influencing others, the key skill differentiating great leaders, negotiators, salespeople and team members.

Outcomes versus relationships

Miller suggests people need to balance outcomes and relationships in getting what they want. If you focus too much on the outcomes, you hurt relationships. And, if you focus too much on relationships, you may not get to the outcomes you need. He notes this balance is an art and getting it right is different in different cultures around the world.

Selling

Miller suggests a "Must – Trust – Now – How" framework for selling. Your prospects must have a need or desire for what you're selling (from their U Perspective.). They must trust you can deliver. They must believe the time is right now. And they must know how to make it happen (and afford it.)

Convince – Collaborate - Create

One of Miller's more powerful frameworks plays off the intersection of convince, collaborate and create. Convincing is about demonstrating that your offering is something they already care about and want. This is subjective and emotional. Collaborating is a rational, interest-based,

---

[61] From George Bradt's June 26, 2018 Forbes.com article, "How Other-Focused Leaders Influence While Self-Focused Leaders Negotiate"

problem-solving approach. This is more objective. Creating is about changing the structure of interactions to get to different results.

CONVINCE

- Demonstrate offering is something they already care about and want (subjective/emotional)
- Anchoring
- Legitimacy
- Active listening
- Purposeful questioning
- Delivering the message

COLLABORATE

- Rational interest-based problem-solving approach (objective)
- Make it a better deal (Win-win negotiating)
- Develop relationships
- Leverage relationships
- Determine interests
- Problem-solving
- Taking advantage of value differences

CREATE

- Change the structure of interaction
- Examine assumptions
- Explore alternates
- Try different things
- Change the people
- Create new paradigms

Negotiating versus Influencing

Miller describes how negotiators sit on opposite sides of the table making trade-offs and compromises to get the best outcome for themselves or the people they represent. Win-win negotiating is the best they can do as that gives them both a winning outcome and preserves a winning relationship.

Someone influencing another sits on the same side of the table as they do. They're not keeping score, but helping the person they are influencing do what's best for them.

While self-focused leaders can discipline themselves to influence at times, it does not come naturally. Their natural default is to negotiate. And when they are influencing, they are doing so because it is ultimately in their own best interests to do so.

Influencing is an other-focused leader's natural default. For other-focused leaders, Miller's U Perspective is not a technique, it's how they think. They begin with others' U Perspective not to get what they want themselves, but rather to help the other get what they want.

As George suggested in an earlier article, this is why the world needs more other-focused leaders.

While each individual balances doing good for others, doing things they are good at, and doing good for themselves differently, those that care more about doing good for others naturally attract like-minded followers and inspire, enable and empower them to do their absolute best together to realize a meaningful and rewarding shared purpose. Other focused BRAVE leaders:

- Play where they and their teams can do the most good for others.
- Care about what matters to the people they are trying to impact and seek to understand why it matters to them.
- Pull together the combined strengths of others, knowing that the world needs three types of leaders: artistic, scientific and interpersonal.
- Enable others to communicate.
- Strive for impact on others

Arranged Marriages -- Working with Difficult Teammates You Didn't Choose[62] **

High performing teams do their absolute best together to realize a meaningful and rewarding shared purpose. When individuals are put together without their own choosing, they can accelerate joint progress by

---

[62] From George Bradt's Oct 11, 2017 Forbes.com article, on "Arranges Marriages – Working with Difficult Teammates You Didn't Choose"

learning each other's stories, rallying around shared purpose and building relationships by helping each other and being open to help.

Astronaut Cady Coleman spoke with George about how she and her crewmates did exactly this leading up to and on their six-month mission on the Space Station. Most of their conversation took place in a car between 4:00 and 5:00 in the morning on their way down from HATCH - which is the closest George will ever come to a descent from space.

Learn Each Other's Stories

Cady was an astronaut for 24 years. She and the other NASA astronauts grew up together, trained together and knew each other well. But her 2010 crew was made up of Dmitri Kondratyev from Russia, Paolo Nespoli from Italy and her. Cady used their training time as back-ups for another mission to get to know Dmitri and Paolo's stories.

Dmitri was an ambitious career-focused professional who preferred to keep to himself and follow orders through the chain of command. When Cady learned that the three of them were going to be the primary crew for the following mission and told Dmitri. He told her "We get our news in an official way." But Cady had also learned that she and "Dima" shared a deep love of family, and used that to see beyond his serious demeanor.

Paolo was more social. Paolo was married to a Russian woman, loved food, and was able to bridge the gap between Cady and Dmitri's worlds

Rally Around the Mission

The one thing these three people from different backgrounds unquestioningly agreed on was that the mission was more important than any of their differences. While they each had their own areas of expertise and responsibilities, there were times when close collaboration was mission-critical. There could be no daylight or starlight between them during launch, docking, reentry or crisis situations.

As the most experienced crewmember, when Cady became concerned that their crisis preparation training wasn't going well enough, she pushed to have the three of them do a short National Outdoor Leadership School (NOLS) program. Even though Dmitri had other commitments, he bowed to the mission's needs

On the other hand, when Cady realized that Dmitri was less accepting of suggestions from her than he was to suggestions from his fellow male crewmember, she bowed to the mission's needs and routed her suggestions through Paolo.

Build Relationships by Helping and Being Open to Help

Paolo's mother unexpectedly died while they were on their mission. Cady did the calculations and arranged for the crew to have a moment of silence while they were passing over Italy at the time of Paolo's mother's funeral service.

Cady makes people feel better about themselves by helping and being open to help. At HATCH, Cady gave a talk about her journey. One of her cabin mates, Katy Yam, helped her prepare. In addition to her ground-breaking work with artificial intelligence at Element AI, Katy produces and curates TEDx Montreal.

Cady described Katy's coaching as "a magical couple of hours…gave me new ways of thinking…meant the world to me." For her part, Katy cited helping Cady as one of the highlights of her HATCH experience. She told us "I just coached an astronaut! I was happy that my comments could help her better connect with the HATCH community."

Implications on Earth

Learn your teammates' stories. Understand their personal histories. Appreciate their strengths. And respect how they feel about different things.

Anchor everything in a shared purpose. Make sure everyone agrees on the mission, vision and guiding principles.

Help each other and be open to help. This is essential in building relationships in general and in doing your absolute best together at points of inflection like the onboarding of a new team member, the launch of a major initiative or moments of crisis.

BRAVE Creative Briefs

Creative briefs are useful to give people the information they need to complete specific creative projects. Getting all the stakeholders aligned around a well-structured creative brief can save all sorts of disconnects, false starts and re-work on any creative project.

BRAVE creative briefs begin with a project description/overview.

Think through and lay out the opportunity, approach, output, timing, and logistics as well as guidelines regarding decision-making; resources including people, budget and operational tools; accountabilities including milestones and timing; consequences including how to leverage the win.

It is particularly important to align expectations around five project questions (which by now should look a lot like the five core BRAVE questions):

1. Where to play?
2. What matters and why?
3. How to win?
4. How to connect?
5. What impact?

ENVIRONMENT - Where to play?

> First, describe the **context**. What we know about customers, collaborators, capabilities, competitors and conditions. (What?) Then lay out **insights** drawn from the contextual data (So what?)

VALUES - What matters and why?

> Clarify the organization's overall **purpose** (Why?) and **objective** (What) as well as how this project fits within that and helps move things in that direction. (e.g. to (mission) so that (vision) occurs.)

ATTITUDE - How to win?

Then lay out the strategy: broad choices (How?)

Begin with organization's over-arching and commercial/marketing strategies including value proposition and posture/cultural tenet (e.g. innovation, discipline, perseverance, agility.)

Lay out the positioning: target, frame of reference, benefit, support/attributes – permission to believe, brand character/attitude/voice.

RELATIONSHIPS - How to connect?

This section lays out the mandatory elements focusing on the few critical elements that will drive the connection with the target audience. These could include components like visuals, selling idea, look, voice, communication points, information, as well as media and channels.

BEHAVIORS - What impact?

Finally, clarify the desired response: How the target will move through AIDA (Aware – Interest – Desire – Action) after experiencing the creative.

BRAVE CREATIVE BRIEF

PROJECT DESCRIPTION: Opportunity, approach, output, timing, logistics as well as guidelines regarding decision-making; resources including people, budget and operational tools; accountabilities including milestones and timing; consequences including how to leverage the win.

ENVIRONMENT - Where to play?
> Context: Customers, collaborators, capabilities, competitors and conditions. Insights drawn from the contextual data (So what?)

VALUES - What matters and why?
> Objective including the organization's overall purpose (Why?) and objective (What?) as well as how this project fits within that and helps move things in that direction.

ATTITUDE - How to win?
> Strategy: Broad choices (How?).
> Organization's over-arching strategy and commercial or marketing strategy including value proposition.
> Positioning: target, frame of reference, benefit, support/attributes – permission to believe, brand character/attitude/voice.

RELATIONSHIPS - How to connect?
> Mandatory elements focused on the few critical elements that will drive the connection with the target audience. These could include components like visuals, selling idea, look, voice, communication points, information as well as media and channels.

BEHAVIORS - What impact?
> Desired response: How the target will move through AIDA (Aware - Interest/understand - Desire/believe - Action) after experiencing the creative.

Milestone Management

Let's make sure we're all dealing with the same definitions:

Objectives: Broadly defined, qualitative performance requirements.
Goals: The quantitative measures of the objectives that define success.
Strategies: Broad choices around how the team will achieve its objectives.
Milestones: Checkpoints along the way to achieving objectives and goals.

The power of milestones is that they let you know how you're doing along the way and give you the opportunity to make adjustments. They also give you the comfort to let your team run toward the goal without your involvement, as long as the milestones are being reached as planned.

You might evaluate your team's journey to a goal like this:

Worst case	Team misses a goal and doesn't know why.
Bad	Team misses a goal and knows why.
Okay	Team misses a milestone but adjusts to make overall goal.
Good	Team anticipates risk and adjusts to make key milestones.
Best	Team hits all milestones on the way to goal . . . (unlikely.)

Imagine that you set a goal of getting from London to Paris in five-and-a-half hours. Now imagine that you choose to drive.

You set off on your journey. It takes you 45 minutes to get from central London to the outskirts of London. Thirty minutes after that, you wonder, "How's the trip going so far?" You have no clue.

You might be on track. You might be behind schedule. But it's early in the trip so you probably think that you can make up time later if you need to. So you're not worried.

If, on the other hand, you had set the following milestones, you would be thinking differently:

- Central London to outskirts of London: 30 minutes.
- Outskirts of London to Folkestone: 70 minutes.
- Channel Crossing: load: 20 minutes; cross: 20 minutes; unload: 20 minutes.
- Calais to Paris: three hours.

If you had set a milestone of getting to the outskirts of London in 30 minutes and it took you 45 minutes, you would know you were behind schedule. Knowing that you were behind schedule, you could then take action on alternative options. The milestone would make you immediately aware of the need to adjust to still reach your overall goal.

You and your team are going to miss milestones. It is not necessary to hit all your milestones. What is essential is that you and your team have put in place a mechanism to identify reasonable milestones so that you have checkpoints that allow you to anticipate and adjust along the way.

Note you'll want to track different levels of work at different frequencies, giving you more senior leaders more leeway. Something like this:

- **Strategic Priorities**: Reconfirm annually, track and adjust quarterly.
- **Programs** to deliver strategic priorities: Track monthly.
- **Projects** delivering parts of programs: Track weekly.
- **Tasks** delivering parts of projects: Manage daily or more frequently.

Manage Milestone Updates with a Three-Step Process

Deploying a mutually supportive team-based follow-up system helps everyone improve performance versus goals. Organizations that have deployed this process in their team meetings have seen dramatic improvements in team performance – especially with a milestone process project manager. Follow these three steps as well as the prep and post instructions laid out here and in Tool 5.7 and you'll be well on your way to ensuring that the team achieves their desired results on time.

Prep: Circulate individual milestone updates to the team to read before each meeting so you can take update sharing and reporting off the agenda, while still deploying a disciplined process to make sure that information flows where it needs to go. Managers often skip this step much to the team's detriment. It seems like an easy process to put in place, but we've heard every reason in the book as to why it has not been implemented. (In others' books. In our book, there's no excuse for not implementing.)

Usually there are some logistic protocols that need to be established, tracking method choices and time frames established for submitting and distribution of information before the process can begin…Make these choices as soon as practical. You must require that everyone complete the update and pre-meeting review on time. If you allow excuses here, the rest of the process takes a hit.

Yes, it can be a pain to get it started, but once it is embedded as a team expectation, you'll be thankful that you endured the brief period of pain.

Step 1.
Use the first half of each meeting for each team member to headline wins, learning, and areas in which the person needs help from other team members, but do not work through items at this point.

Discussing items here reinforces a first-come, first-served mentality where the people who share later in the order tend to get squeezed for time. The "help from other team members" is often the most important part of the meeting. Each of these items should be captured. It's a good idea to keep a set time limit for each individual update. Those who tend to be long-winded might not like it, but the rest of the participants will appreciate it. A tight and controlled limit goes a long way to making the meetings more dynamic.

Step 2.
Pause at the meeting's halfway point to prioritize items for discussion so the team can discuss items in the right priority instead of first-come, first-served. These won't necessarily be the universally most important items because some items should be worked with a different group or subset of the team. You should make note of those items in the meeting, but defer them to another meeting where the full and proper group can address them. Instead, give priority to the most important items for this team to work on as a team, at this time. Tend to give priority to items that are off-target, or in danger, or to areas where help is needed. Develop a list in descending order of priority.

Step 3.
Use the second part of the meeting to discuss, in order, the priority list you determined to be the overall team's most important issues and opportunities. The expectation is that the team won't get through all the items. That's okay because you're working the most important items first (which is why you paused to prioritize items.) This is the time to figure out how to adjust as a team to make the most important goals, all the while reinforcing predetermined decision rights.

Post:
Defer other items to the next meeting or to a separate meeting. Update the tracking reports with any changes or new directions. Communicate major shifts to those key stakeholders who need to know.

BRAVE Tip 1

Anticipation is the key: at first, milestones will go from "on track" to "oops we missed" with no steps in between. You'll know the process is working well when people are surfacing areas they "might miss" if they don't get help from others. Focus your love and attention on these "might miss" items to get the team to help. It will make people feel good about surfacing issues and will encourage them to bring future issues to the group for help.

BRAVE Tip 2

Banish the first-come, first-served mentality. This milestone process is easy to deploy for disciplined people and teams. It is hard for less disciplined people because they want to work items first-come, first-served. Resist that. Follow the process. You'll learn to love it. (Well, maybe not love it, but you will appreciate it. It will strengthen your team.)

BRAVE Tip 3

Integrate across instead of managing down: The milestone meetings are great forums for making connections across groups. The further you rise in the organization, the more time you'll spend integrating across and the less time you'll spend managing down. Most don't like to be tightly managed or have their decision rights compromised, but everyone appreciates improved information flows and linking projects and priorities across groups.

MILESTONE MANAGEMENT

Milestone Management Process

Leader conducts a weekly or bi-weekly milestones management meeting with their team.

Prior to Milestones Management Meetings:

Each team member submits their updates.

Designated person compiles and circulates updated milestones in advance of the meeting.

At Milestones Management Meetings

First part of the meeting:

Each team member gives a five-minute update in the following format: most important wins, most important learnings, areas where they need help.

Midpoint of the meeting:

The leader orders topics for discussion in order of priority.

Second part of the meeting:

Group discusses priority topics in order, spending as much time as necessary on each topic.

The remaining topics are deferred to the next milestones management meeting or a separate meeting. Key items are updated and communicated.

Weekly Milestone Report					
Strategic Priority	**Activity**	**Owner**	**Date Due**	**Status**	**Details/Outcome/Help Needed**
Process:				Not started	
Prior to meeting:				Complete	
- Each team member submits their updates				On target	
- Updates compiled and circulated prior to the meeting				Tracking	
				Lagging	

Copyright© PrimeGenesis®. To customize this document, download Tools 5.7 and 5.7b from the BRAVE Leadership page on www.onboardingtools.com.

Royal Caribbean's CEO Exemplifies How to Leverage Milestones[63]

Tracking milestones is not a revolutionary business idea. However, the idea of using them as a team-building tool is new to most leaders and their teams. Royal Caribbean's CEO, Richard Fain, fully appreciates the power of milestones and exemplifies how other leaders can utilize them to keep projects on track and recognize employee achievements.

Milestones for Project Management

Fain's emphasis on milestones is not a surprise, as ship builders have been leveraging milestones' emotional impact for millennia. Ship builders celebrate "keel laying" as the formal start of construction, naming, stepping the mast (accompanied by placing coins under the mast for good luck,) christening (accompanied by breaking a bottle of champagne over the bow,) a whole range of trials, "sail away", hand over, and my personal favorite – onboarding the new captain.

As Fain explained to me,

> *"If you don't establish early on key milestones – long-term milestones rather than the short-term milestones – you get caught in the 'next week' syndrome. I can't think of a project that we are doing or have done (during which we do not) get to a key point and everybody says 'We're going to know so much more next week or the week after.' And so the focus shifts to next week or the week after and we all desperately wait for that period. Meanwhile the longer-term milestone goes by the wayside.*
>
> *So what we tend to do is say we need to know where we're going. We need to know what we expect to have at the end. And so we talk a lot about our end point rather than the waypoints."*

Milestones for Team Building

What Fain does particularly well is leverage milestones both as a way to keep big projects on track – like building a ship, a new computer system, or a major marketing program – and to keep smaller projects on track. They also provide him with excuses to encourage all involved along the way. He goes to major events. He participates in new ship trials so he can experience the excitement of how the ship performs. Then he shares that excitement with others in his meetings, talks, videos, blog, and all forms of communication.

---

[63] From George Bradt's March 23, 2011 Forbes.com article, "Royal Caribbean's CEO Exemplifies How to Leverage Milestones"

In an interview with Knowledge@Wharton, Fain talked about "letting people know you care is of surpassing value." The links with his approach to milestones come through. He's built a team of people that try to surpass – and he gives them milestones to beat. He knows that people value recognition – and he leverages milestone ceremonies to recognize their achievements whether it's the first time people can actually walk on board and see a ship, or the first look at the prototype of a new computer system.

Royal Caribbean likes to build models so people can see and touch tangible things and know what they are going to do. They model staterooms, software, and marketing materials. When a project gets to a certain point, they give it a name. *"It's interesting how giving that project a name galvanizes people around it – because it makes it more tangible to them."*

One of its big projects was the creation of a central gathering area on the ship "Oasis of the Seas." This area – which is aptly named Central Park — is located in the middle of the ship and opens to the sky for five decks. To celebrate the design, Royal Caribbean created a full-size model of part of this open space in the massive hangar-like building where parts of the ship were being built in Finland. Also, the company treated the whole team to an alfresco fine dining experience so they could celebrate the space.

"It was a magical evening …We were having a lovely cruise dinner in Finland (in early Spring – when it's still cold outside)… It made us all realize how special the space would be and that it was worthy of the effort to really make sure that not only was the overall space good, but that all the details were perfect."

Once they know you care, then you can challenge them. As Fain said in a recent interview with Adam Bryant for the New York Times, *"My experience is that people love to be challenged. If the challenge is reasonable, or even slightly unreasonable, they love it and they rise to the occasion. There's just no question. People love to be challenged and they love to show off their skills and talents."* Aggressive, but doable milestones create just such a challenge.

Establish a Process to Track Milestones

Compiling milestones is a waste of time if you do not have an efficient, effective and clear process in place to track them – and avoid the "next week" syndrome. Define them and begin tracking and managing to them immediately. Use the process to establish and reinforce expected team norms.

1. Get milestones in place.
2. Track them and manage them as a team on a frequent and regular basis.
3. Implement a milestone management process with a particular emphasis on solving problems and celebrating wins – as a team (with your own version of a lovely al fresco cruise dinner in a warehouse.)

Management Cadence Framework

Focus on strategic, organizational and operational issues and opportunities with appropriate governance and culture as your foundation.

The Strategic Process is about the creation and allocation of the right resources to the right places in the right way over time. It comes from the Greek "strategos" and is the art of the general, arranging forces <u>before</u> battle. Think in terms of broad choices for how to achieve objectives.
>Plan annually
>Implement through organizational and operational processes

The Organizational Process is about people - acquiring, developing, encouraging, planning and transitioning them. You can't get from strategy to execution without people.
>Plan annually: Future Capabilities, Succession, Contingencies
>Implement: Programs, projects and tasks to acquire, develop, encourage and transition people

The Operational Process is about making things happen, tactics. This comes from the Greek "taktikos," the art of deploying forces <u>during</u> battle. This includes tasks that roll up into projects that in turn roll up into programs to design, build, sell, deliver or experience products or services.
>Plan: Annual operating plan with monthly and quarterly reviews and updates – and perhaps rolling quarterly.
>Plan programs and projects as appropriate.

Implement:
> Tasks: Performed and managed real time/daily
> Projects: Interdependent tasks rolled up into projects tracked and managed weekly
> Programs: Interdependent projects rolled up into programs tracked and managed monthly

The Governance Process is about ensuring compliance with laws, regulations and policies. Note this process is generally owned by the board.

Culture is made up of behaviors, relationships, attitudes, values and the environment.

Tool 5.8
Management Cadence

Q1 Talent Review
Q2 Strategic
Q3 Future Capability, Succession and Contingency Planning
Q4 Operating Plan | Business Review & adjustment

And each quarter: Business Review & adjustment
Priority Programs (monthly)/Projects (weekly)

Rolling quarterly planning. Each quarter:
- PRIOR QUARTER – Capture key learnings – implications for future.
- CURRENT QUARTER – Update progress. Understand potential misses. Realign resources to optimize overall results.
- NEXT QUARTER – Finalize goals. Ensure resources in place.
- TWO QUARTERS OUT – Nearly finalize goals. Ensure longer lead-time items being worked.
- THREE to FOUR QUARTERS OUT – Update general plans including things that need to be done more than four quarters out to be ready to implement in planning horizon.
- FIVE to SIX QUARTERS OUT – Initial targets set.

BRAVE Customer Experience

Others can take your ideas and hire away your people. But they can't duplicate your culture. They can copy your product or service. But they can never match the emotional connections you make with your customers or guests. This is why it's worth taking a BRAVE approach to customer experience, working through behaviors, relationships, attitudes, values and environment in this (different) order, with these main points:

Values:	Surprise and delight each individual customer or guest with new ways of experiencing who you are.
Attitude:	Over deliver at every step in every way every day.
Environment:	Set the stage across all five senses (look, feel, sound, smell, taste.)
Behaviors:	Prioritize human interactions.
Relationships:	Make and enable extraordinary emotional connections, shared stories and memories.

Values:

What matters most is surprising and delighting each individual customer or guest with new ways of experiencing who you are. This is about leveraging your foundational strengths to exceed their hopes and needs and make them feel important, appreciated and wonderful. Embed this and why it matters to your customers or guests as a foundation of your culture.

For example, Disney is about bringing happiness to the world's families.

Attitude:

Choose to over deliver at every step across systems, procedures, touch points, interactions and, ultimately, experiences, "optimizing the mundane." By definition, over delivering requires empowering people to go beyond the norm so they can say "yes" to customer or guest requests and think in terms of service recovery – overcompensating for mistakes.

Disney cast members are taught that the most asked question in the Magic Kingdom is "What time is the 3:00 parade?" What guests asking that really want to know is if the parade is running that day, what time it will get to where they are, whether they are in a good position to see the parade, or something else.

Environment:

Set the stage. Make things practically perfect in every way that each customer or guest sees, feels, hears, smells and tastes their own personal and collective experiences.

Disney sets its stage across all five senses. The Magic Kingdom is Disney movies brought to life. As guests move through each "set", the architecture, plants, costumes, sound effects, music, aroma, food choices and texture change accordingly. And every day someone paints any grass brown spots green before the parks open.

Behaviors:

Human interactions are the real differentiator. You must get these right to earn the opportunity to build and enable relationships. Codify your standards, policies and guidelines to minimize behavioral downsides and enable upsides.

Disney fills its parks with street sweepers, ostensibly picking up litter. But their main job is interacting with guests to enhance their experience.

Relationships:

The real magic is in the emotional connections. The stage and your behaviors are necessary, but not sufficient. The most gratifying experiences always include extraordinary emotional connections and stories. This is why you must inspire, enable, prompt, guide, support, amplify and reinforce your customer or guests' interactions, connections and stories with your product, service and community to create memories they want to experience again.

One guest arrived late at a Disney hotel. The receptionist asked if he'd had a long day. He had. She asked if he'd eaten. He had not. As the kitchen was about to close, she arranged for it to stay open, had someone call his room as soon as he got there to take his order and followed up twenty minutes later to make sure he'd gotten everything he might have wanted.

BRAVE Onboarding

One of the trickiest personal points of inflection is onboarding into a new leadership role or merging teams. Having a framework, process and set of tools leading up to and through your first 100 days can help you to meet these challenges and propel you down the path to success. It's so important that we've written a whole book on this, "The New Leader's 100-Day Action Plan" with its companion series "Executive Onboarding."

The fundamental concept is that you must converge into the organization or team before trying to evolve it. And the four main ideas are:

1. **Get a head start**. Day One is a critical pivot point for people moving into new roles or merging teams. In both situations, you can accelerate progress by getting a head start and hitting the ground running. Preparation in the days and weeks leading up to Day One breeds confidence; and a little early momentum goes a long way.

2. **Manage the message.** Everything communicates. People read things into everything you say and do and don't say and don't do. You're far better off choosing and guiding what others see and hear, and when they see and hear it, rather than letting happenstance or others make those choices for you. Start this process with your current best thinking on your organizing concept before Day One and adjust steadfastly as you go along.

3. **Set direction. Build the team.** The first 100 days is the best time to put in place the basic building blocks of a cohesive, high-performing team. You will fail if you try to create the organization's imperative yourself, without the support and buy-in of your team. As team leader, your own success is inextricably linked to the success of the team as a whole.

4. **Sustain momentum. Deliver results**. Although the first 100 days are a sprint to jump- start communication, team building and core practices, it's all for naught if you then sit back and watch things happen. You must evolve your leadership, practices and culture to keep fueling the fires you sparked and deliver ongoing results.

Filling in and implementing tool 5.11, BRAVE Onboarding, will give you a good start on these four ideas.

BRAVE ONBOARDING

This BRAVE personal onboarding planning exercise (distinct from business planning) will give you a head start with your best current thinking. You don't know enough to get this right the first time. But, if you don't think in advance and create some testable hypotheses to set up your own directed learning, you'll be on the back foot just responding to everyone else. So, fill in what you know. Accept your gaps. And get going to start building relationships on the way to converging into your new organization before trying to evolve it.

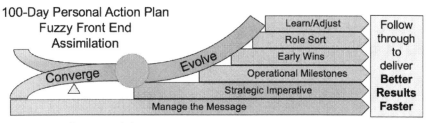

[preparation/learning/plan]

Environment:

Understand what you're getting yourself into by digging into the historical context, business environment and recent results, and where the organization currently chooses to play.

Lay out the organization's historical context including the founder's vision if applicable.

Describe the organization's recent results.

Describe Customers, Collaborators, Capabilities, Competitors and Conditions (see 5Cs tool)

- **Customers**: First line, customer chain, end users, influencers.

- **Collaborators**: Suppliers, allies, government/community leaders.

- **Capabilities**: Human, operational, financial, technical, key assets.

- **Competitors**: Direct, indirect, potential.

- **Conditions**: Social/demographic, political/govt/regulatory, economic, market, health, climate.

Complete SWOT (with SWOT tool)
- **Strengths**: Internal to organization - things we do better

- **Weaknesses**: Internal to organization - things we do worse

- **Opportunities**: External to organization - things to capitalize on

- **Threats:** External to organization - things to worry about

- **Key Leverage Points:** Opportunities > < Strengths (where play to win)

- **Business Implications:** Threats > < Weaknesses (where play not to lose)

- **Sustainable Competitive Advantages:** Leverage points to sustain over time

Think through and record implications from these re where to focus first.

Values:
Understand the organization's current mission, vision, and guiding principles so you know what matters and why to the organization at this point.

- **Mission**: Why we are here, why we exist, what business we are in.

- **Vision**: Future picture—what we want to become, where we are going.

- **Guiding principles**: Beliefs & principles to guide attitudes, relationships & behaviors.

Attitude:
Understand the organization's current strategy, priorities and culture to set up how to win.

- **Strategy**: The single overarching choice guiding resource choices.

- **Priorities**: Resource choices in line with that strategy (predominant, superior, strong, above average, good enough, not do/ally/outsource)

- **Culture**: Behaviors, relationships, attitudes, values, environment.

Relationships:
Lay out your current best thinking on how to connect by working through stakeholders, message and initial actions to get a head start, manage your message and start building your team.

Fill in the names/titles of the few most critical stakeholders:

Up: your boss, their boss, and any other people that can tell you what to do

Across: internal peers, external and internal customers and suppliers

Down: direct reports, perhaps some indirect reports

Former: (if promoted from within) up, across, down stakeholders from former role

Lay out headline organizing concept and communication plan:

Platform for change: Note what will make your audience realize they need to change.

Vision: Lay out a brighter future – in which your audience can picture themselves.

Call to action: Note actions the audience can take.

Headline: The one bumper sticker / organizing concept for your message. (1-5 words) Your organizing concept is the strategic core idea you execute in your message and communication points to impact how others feel.

Message points: The three main points.

Amplifiers: Note the people and things that will convey and amplify your message.

Media: Lay out which media to use.

Steps: Note the steps of your communication plan.

Plan fuzzy front end/pre-start steps

Personal set up: Note things to get family set and basic office accommodations.

Jump-start learning: Information to gather and digest across
1. *Technical learning* - the company's products, customers, technologies, and systems
2. *Cultural learning* - behavioral, relationship, attitudinal norms, values and environment
3. *Political learning* - how decisions are made, who has the power to make them, and whose support you will need. => Shared reality/unwritten rules

Conversations: The few most critical stakeholders to meet live/by phone pre day one.

Announcement Cascade: Who will hear what, when, how, before announcement; how announcement will be made; and who will hear what, when, how after announcement. (Emotionally impacted: 1:1, Directly: small group, Indirect: large group, Less: mass)

Day One/early days: Specific actions for day one - whom meet, when, what forum. What signals to send/how to reinforce message. Complete the same for the early days.

Pivot: How to pivot from converging to evolving in creating a high performing team.

Behaviors:
Lay out your current best thinking to jump-start strategic, operational, organizational processes

Strategic   *Burning Imperative:* likely a workshop to co-create and commit to a compelling imperative together (either live or virtually,) leading to a business plan. Use consultative approach if you do not have confidence in your team. Fill in approach (workshop or consult, live or virtual) and target date (likely by day 30):

Operational: *Milestones:* jump-starting your operational process – likely by day 45. This is the heart of your business plan – what's getting done by whom, when. Fill in start date:

                        Early Wins: must jump-start in first 60 days to deliver by end of six months. Fill in start date:

Organizational: *Roles:* pick date to make decisions about your team (then implement over time.)

Communication: Other critical communication steps including daily/weekly/monthly/quarterly/annual meeting flows to update milestones, business reviews, strategic, operating, organizational plans:

Self: *Accelerator:* Self-assessment + stakeholder feedback to course correct and sustain momentum.

Acquisition Integration

We know that 83% of mergers fail. We keep doing them because the upside to success is so huge. That success comes only when the vision, values and integration are right. While the CEO must own the vision and strategy and values and culture, having an integration leader own the integration process reduces risk and accelerates progress. This section suggests a BRAVE approach for you as that integration leader working through Behaviors, Relationships, Attitudes, Values and the Environment from the outside-in.

- **Environment** – Understand the context and type of integration you're leading.
- **Values** – Clarify what matters and why to the CEO and other key stakeholders.
- **Attitude** – Clarify choices around strategy, culture, organization, operations, and your own role over time.
- **Relationships** – Build mutual trust and confidence with the top leadership team, the integration team, and the combined organization's future leadership.
- **Behaviors** – Accelerate to future capabilities.

Environment/Context

Start by understanding the type of integration you're leading.

1. Acquired company A folded into acquiring company B (the default approach)
2. Acquiring company B folded into acquired company A (where it makes sense)
3. Merging company A and B together to form something completely new (more complex)
4. Keeping A and B separate while adding strong links between the two (less synergistic)

Note these are not all or nothing choices. You may choose to combine different parts of different companies differently.

Values/What matters and why

You don't get to decide what matters and why. Mission (why,) vision (what,) and values are determined by the CEO, board, and/or owners. But you can't lead the integration until you understand what they really care about. Keep laddering down by asking them why things matter and laddering up by asking what the impact will be until you understand their thinking in depth.

Attitude/Choices

Mergers are points of inflection for all involved. The fundamental strategy choice across design, produce, service, or deliver drives every other choice. Your new, combined organization should focus on one and only one of the four boxes below. There's more on this in my article on accelerating through a strategic inflection point, but pay particular attention to the cultural integration, looking at the same four types of integration laid out in Environment above.

The M&A Leadership Council's Mark Herdon suggests the role of the integration leader is to manage chaos as key point of contact, accelerate process by helping executive staff manage, architect success by providing focus and direction, and personally drive the change on major issues.

This role is unique in that it's part interim leader, part deputy, part program manager, and part link between the current leadership team, integration management team and future leadership team. The role ends when the integration is complete. Think about where you want to go next. Do you want to be part of the future leadership team, go back to the parent organization, move on to the next integration? That will affect how you think about the various relationships.

Relationships/Connecting

In times of change or crisis, people retreat back down Maslow's hierarchy. Their first question is always, "What about me?" Remember this as you build your relationships with the CEO and top leadership, integration leadership (including the board, owners and PE leadership,) and broader future leadership team. As Theodore Roosevelt said, "No one cares how much you know until they know how much you care." You have to build relationships before you can lead anyone.

In particular, pay attention to the CEO – especially if you were dropped in on them. In that case, invest in building trust in the face of possible distrust or resentment. Jump-shift your loyalties immediately. 1) Disengage from your previous situation – especially if you were part of the board or ownership group; 2) Engage with the CEO as your new boss; and 3) Do what is required to accelerate the integration's progress – in that order.

Behaviors/Impact

Ultimately acquisition integration is about accelerating to future capabilities.

1. **Imperative.** Start with the end state. Get all aligned around the imperative: mission, vision, values, core strategies.
2. **Future organizational capabilities.** Those strategies will inform the future organizational capabilities you'll need to implement them.
3. **Current reality.** Take a hard look at the capabilities you've got in both the current acquiring organization and acquired organization.
4. **Bridge the gaps.** Now operationalize the change. Build the required cross-functional and cross-entity integration teams. Lay out plans and milestones on the way to the integration. Manage them on a regular basis, picking, delivering and highlighting early wins along the way to give the team confidence in itself.
5. **Communicate** up, across, and down on a regular basis. You can't over-communicate in an integration. The more people know, the better.

What type of integration are you leading?
1. Acquired company A folded into acquiring company B (the default approach)
2. Acquiring company B folded into acquired company A (where it makes sense)
3. Merging company A and B together to form something completely new (more complex)
4. Keeping A and B separate while adding strong links between the two (less synergistic)

Are there any parts of the organizations that should be integrated differently?

The new organization's mission (why)?

Vision (what success looks like)?

Values (that will not be compromised along the way)?

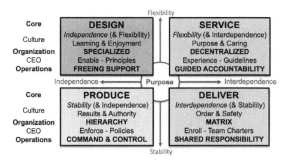

Fundamental choice (Develop – Produce – Distribute – Serve)?

Overriding culture?

Type of organization?

CEO's role?

Operational approach?

Your next role after integration leader?

Stakeholders up, across at both organizations and down?

Their concerns and issues?

Your fundamental headline message/organizing concept? (Platform for change | Vision of a brighter future | Call to action => headline message/organizing concept)

Contact plan for key stakeholders?

How align all around imperative? When?

How align all around required future organizational capabilities? When?

How complete assessment of current reality at both organizations? When?

How build out cross-functional and cross-entity integration teams? When?

How develop action plans and milestones? When?

Management cadence?

When choose early wins? When deliver?

Communication cadence?

Crisis Management

Leading through a crisis is about inspiring, enabling and empowering others to get things vaguely right quickly, and then adapt along the way - with clarity around direction, leadership and roles.

This plays out in three steps of a disciplined iteration in line with an organization's overall purpose:

1. PREPARE IN ADVANCE: The better you have anticipated possible scenarios, the more prepared you are, the more confidence you will have when crises strike.

2. REACT TO EVENTS: The reason you prepared is so that you all can react quickly and flexibility to the situation you face. Don't over-think this. Do what you prepared to do.

3. BRIDGE THE GAPS. In a crisis, there is inevitably a gap between the desired and current state of affairs. Rectify that by bridging those gaps in the:

   - Situation - implementing a response to the current crisis
   - Response - improving capabilities to respond to future crises
   - Prevention - reducing the risk of future crises happening in the first place

Along the way, keep the ultimate purpose in mind. It needs to inform and frame everything you do over the short, mid and long term as you lead through a crisis instead of merely out of a crisis. Crises change your organization. Be sure the choices you make during crises change you in ways that move you towards your purpose and not away from your core vision and values.

Prepare in advance

   - Establish crisis management protocols, explicitly including early communication protocols.
   - Identify and train crisis management teams (with clear leadership and roles.)
   - Preposition human, financial, and operational resources.

Note preparing in advance is about building general capabilities and capacity – not specific situational knowledge. For the most part, there is a finite set of the most likely, most devastating *types* of crises and disasters that are worth preparing for. Think them through. Run the drills. Capture the general lessons so people can apply them flexibly to the specific situations they encounter. Have resources ready to be deployed when those disasters strike.

Threats may be one or more of the following, often in combination:

- Physical (Top priority. Deal with these first.)
- Reputational (Second priority. Deal with these after physical but before financial threats.)
- Financial (Third priority)

Physical threats and crises may be

- Natural: earthquakes, landslides, volcanic eruptions, floods, cyclones, etc.
- Man-made: stampedes, fires, transport accidents, industrial accidents, oil spills, nuclear explosions/radiation, war, deliberate attacks, etc.

Reputational threats and crisis may flow from physical threats and crisis and how they are handled, or may come from: choices by you or others in your organization, outside interventions, sudden awareness of things already there, etc.

Financial threats come from disruptions in your value chain: supply or product or resources (including cash), manufacturing, selling/demand, distribution, service, etc.

Now, back to three things you should do to prepare.

Establish crisis management protocols. Lay out who's going to do what when in a crisis. In general, you'll want first responders to deal with immediate physical threats to people and property. They should i) secure the scene to eliminate further threats to others and themselves; ii) provide immediate assistance to those hurt or injured or set up a triage system to focus on those that can most benefit from help; iii) trigger your communication protocols.

There are two parts to your communication protocols. Part I protocols deal with physical issues. Part II deal with reputational issues.

Part I protocols spell out who gets informed when (with lots of redundant back-ups built in.) These should have a bias to inform more people faster.

Part II protocols are about formal, external communication. At a minimum, the one, single primary spokesperson (and back-up,) message and communication points should be crystal clear. Three over-arching ideas from the Forbes Agency Council's 13 Golden Rules of PR Crisis Management:

- Develop strong organizational brand culture to ward-off self-inflicted crises and be better ready to deal with others.
- Monitor, plan and communicate, ever on the lookout for potential crises. Then be proactive and transparent, getting ahead of the story and ready for the social media backlash.
- Take responsibility. Own your own crisis in a human way. Seek first to understand, avoiding knee-jerk reactions, apologize, then take action that helps, not fuel the fire.

Identify and train crisis management teams. Protocols are useless if people haven't been trained to apply them. Make sure your first responders are trained in first aid and triage. Make sure your communicators are trained in communicating in a crisis so people know whom to contact when and when to trigger crisis management protocols.

One of the learnings from the Boeing 737 Max crashes is that their crisis management protocols should have been triggered years ago. It seems that some knew there was a potential problem and chose not to deal with it.

Prepositioning human, financial, and operational resources. People need direction, training and resources. Make sure there's a site leader at each of your sites with access to cash. Make sure your first responders have working first-aid kits.

React to events

Our fight or flight instincts evolved to equip us for moments like this. If the team has the capabilities and capacity in place, turn it loose to respond to the events. This is where all the hard work of preparation pays off.

A big part of this is knowing when and how to react without under or over-reacting.

Someone was counterfeiting Coca-Cola fountain syrup. It was safe. No risk to consumers. No reputational risk. Some financial impact. Choose not to react. Hired private investigators. Found the counterfeiters. Shut them down without anyone ever knowing. Well done.

Capper got out of sync, shredding glass shards onto the lip of glass bottles. Clear physical risk to consumers. Shut down the capper. Recalled all product from every retail outlet within 48 hours. Well done.

Handful of school children got sick in school after drinking Coca-Cola. Coca-Cola investigation revealed product was fine. So they did nothing. More children got sick. It turned out preservative from pallets on which Coke cans were stored reacted to the ammonia wash inside Coca-Cola vending machines leading to the illnesses. Classic under-reaction led to massive forced recalls, huge financial and reputational damage.

The story of Procter & Gamble's reaction to its New Orleans' Folger's plant getting destroyed by Hurricane Katrina is a model for how to over-react in the best possible way. Their essential steps included:

- Contacting every employee they could, eventually finding all 550 to be safe.
- Putting $5,000 into every employee's bank accounts immediately to help them deal with short-term issues no questions asked while continuing to pay everyone their full salary during the shut-down.
- Bringing 130 trailers and dining facilities and personal care products to the plant parking lot for temporary housing for those that needed it.
- Flooding the area with people (pun intended) to get the plant back up and running within three weeks.

Bridge the gaps

While first responders should react in line with their training, keep in mind that random, instinctual, uncoordinated actions by multiple groups exacerbate chaos. Stopping everything until excruciatingly detailed situation assessments have been fed into excruciatingly detailed plans that get approved by excruciatingly excessive layers of management leads to things happening too late.

The preferred methodology for what Harrald calls the "integration" phase is to pause to accelerate, get thinking and plans vaguely right quickly, and then get going to bridge the gaps with a combination of discipline (structure, doctrine, process) and agility (creativity, improvisation, adaptability).

Situational questions (Keeping in mind the physical, political, emotional context)

- What do we know, and not know about what happened and its impact (facts)?
- What are the implications of what we know and don't know (conclusions)?
- What do we predict may happen (scenarios)?
- What resources and capabilities do we have at our disposal (assets)? Gaps?
- What aspects of the situation can we turn to our advantage?

Objectives and Intent

Armed with answers to those questions, think through and choose the situational objectives and intent. What are the desired outcomes of leading through the crisis? What is the desired end- state? This is a critical component of direction and a big deal.

Priorities

The Red Cross provides relief to victims of disasters. In doing that, the prioritization of shelter, food, water, medicine and emotional support varies by the type of disaster. If someone's home is destroyed by a fire in the winter, shelter takes precedence. On the other hand, if a reservoir gets contaminated, the critical priority is getting people clean water.

These examples illustrate the importance of thinking through the priorities for each individual situation – and each stage of a developing crisis. The choices for isolating, containing, controlling and stabilizing the immediate situation likely will be different than the priorities for the mid-term response, getting resources in the right place and then delivering the required support over time. Those in turn will be different from the priorities involved in repairing the damage from the crisis or disaster and preventing its re-occurrence.

Get the answer to the question, "where do we focus our efforts first?" and the priority choices clear. And get them communicated to all, perhaps starting with a set of meetings to:

- Recap current situation and needs, and what has already been accomplished (What)
- Agree objectives, intent, priorities and phasing of priorities (So what)
- Agree action plans, milestones, role sort, communication points, plans and protocols (Now what)

Bridge the gap between the desired and current state.

Support team members in implementing plans while gathering more information concurrently.

Complete situation assessment and mid-term prioritization and plans.

Conduct milestone update sessions daily or more frequently as appropriate.

- Update progress on action plans with focus on wins, learning, areas needing help
- Update situation assessment
- Adjust plans iteratively, reinforcing the expectation of continuous adjustment.

Over-communicate at every step of the way to all the main constituencies. Your message and main communication points will evolve as the situation and your information about the situation evolve. This makes the need that much greater for frequent communication updates within the organization, with partner organizations and the public. Funneling as much as possible through one spokesperson will reduce misinformation. Do not underestimate the importance of this.

Your communication should be emotional, rational and inspirational:

- **Emotional**: Connect with your audience by being authentic, relatable, vulnerable and compassionate as you empathize with how the crisis is affecting them personally – Mayfield and Mayfield's empathetic language.[64]

- **Rational**: Lay out the hard facts of the current situation – in detail with a calm, composed, polite and authoritative tone and manner – the first part of the Stockdale Paradox.

- **Inspirational**: Inspire others by thinking ahead, painting an optimistic view of a future they care about, and calling people to practical actions they can take to be part of the solution - instilling confidence in themselves with Mayfield and Mayfield's meaning-making and direction-giving language.

Re-booting through Maslow's Hierarchy

The Covid-19 Pandemic reminded everyone of the long-term effects of a prolonged crisis. Covid-19 reset everyone's progress up Maslow's hierarchy of physiological, safety, belonging, self-esteem, and self-actualization needs. We learned the importance of meeting people where they are moving back up the hierarchy together.[65]

---

[64] Jacqueline and Milton Mayfield, *Leader Communication Strategies - Critical Paths to Improving Employee Commitment* – American Business Review, June 2002

[65] From George Bradt's October 6, 2020 Forbes article on "Helping Employees Manage Through COVID Wave II"

First officer Jeff Skiles was the "pilot in charge" of the airplane that took off, ran into a flock of birds, and lost both its engines. At that point, Captain Chesley Sullenberger chose to take over. With his "My aircraft", followed by Jeff's "Your aircraft", command was passed to "Sully" who safely landed the plane on the Hudson River. Only one pilot can be in charge at a time. Two people trying to steer the same plane at the same time simply does not work.

The same is true for crisis and disaster management. Only one person can be the "pilot in charge" of any effort or component at a time. A critical part of implementation is clarifying and re-clarifying who is doing what, and who is making what decisions at what point – especially as changing conditions dictate changes in roles and decision-making authority within and across organizations. Make sure the hand-offs are as clean as the one on Sully and Skiles' flight.

Bridge the gaps between desired and current response and desired and most recent crisis prevention (improving things and reducing risks for the future)

At the end of the crisis, conduct an after-action review looking at:

- What actually happened? How did that compare with what we expected to happen?
- What impact did we have? How did that compare with our objectives?
- What did we do particularly effectively that we should do again?
- What can we do even better the next time in terms of risk mitigation and response?

This kicks off preparing in advance for the next crisis.[66]

----

[66] Adapted from George Bradt's March 21, 2019 Forbes article, "Learnings from Boeing's 737 Max, Coca-Cola, And Procter & Gamble On Crisis Management

By definition, a crisis results from a major, temporary change. The trap is in managing the crisis itself instead of managing through the crisis. Think in terms of physical safety, reputation and finances – in that order. The fundamental approach is to prepare in advance, react to events and bridge the gaps while keeping in mind that leading through a crisis is about inspiring, enabling and empowering others to get things vaguely right quickly, and then adapt along the way - with clarity around direction, leadership and roles.

1 – Prepare in advance

The better you have anticipated possible threats and scenarios, the more prepared you are, the more confidence you will have when crises strike. The goal is not just to manage out of crises, but to lead through them to help the organization adapt and emerge even stronger than it was going into the crises.

Threats may be:

- Physical (Top priority. Deal with these first.)
- Reputational (Second priority. Deal with these after physical but before financial threats.)
- Financial (Third priority)

Physical threats and crises may be

- Natural: earthquakes, landslides, volcanic eruptions, floods, cyclones, diseases, etc.
- Man-made: stampedes, fires, transport accidents, industrial accidents, oil spills, nuclear explosions/radiation, war, deliberate attacks, etc.

Reputational threats and crisis may flow from physical threats and crisis and how they are handled, or may come from: choices by you or others in your organization, outside interventions, sudden awareness of things already there, etc.

Financial threats come from disruptions in your value chain: supply or product or resources (including cash), manufacturing, selling/demand, distribution, service, etc.

Prepare in advance:

- Establish crisis management protocols, explicitly including early communication protocols.
- Identify and train crisis management teams (with clear leadership and roles.)
- Prepositioning human, financial, and operational resources.

Note preparing in advance is about building general capabilities and capacity – not specific situational knowledge. For the most part, there is a finite set of the most likely, most devastating *types* of crises and disasters that are worth preparing for. Think them through. Run the drills. Capture the general lessons so people can apply them flexibly to the specific situations they encounter. Have resources ready to be deployed when those disasters strike.

2 – React to events

The reason you prepared is so that you all can react quickly and flexibly to the situation you face. Don't over think this. Do what you prepared to do.

Certainly, first responders should react in line with their training. Everyone else should pause to accelerate, get their thinking and plans vaguely right quickly, and then get going to bridge the gaps, iterating and improving as they go.

Determine if you're facing a crisis – with a major and temporary impact.

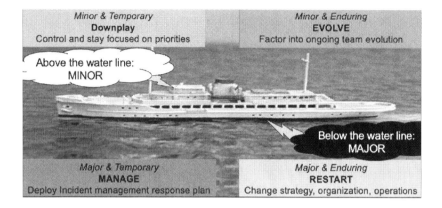

- **Minor change/temporary impact:** Control the damage while staying focused on your priorities.
- **Minor change/enduring impact:** Factor into your ongoing organizational evolution.
- **Major change/enduring impact.** Hit a restart button at this major point of inflection, re-look at your critical relationships, and change your strategy, organization and operations all together, all at the same time.
- **Major change/temporary impact.** This is a crisis or opportunity that must be managed. Deploy the incident management and response plan that you already have in place. (And have it in place ahead of time.)

If it is a crisis, keep going.

SET ORGANIZATION/ROLES:

- **Crisis Management Team:** 5-7 people with diverse functional and varying management perspectives.
- **Communication Lead:** a spokesperson and back-up to assure a definitive information sources, should observe Crisis Management Team meetings

REVISIT PURPOSE:

Recap organization's purpose to ensure everyone has the same long-term view. Mission (why), vision (what), and values (how) must guide everything, including short-term crisis response.

ANALYZE AND AGREE PHYSICAL, POLITICAL, EMOTIONAL CONTEXT:

Context is key. Complete as soon as practical and then update as things change – which they will.

- What do we know, and not know about what happened and its impact? (These are facts, data, things everyone looking at sees the same way.)
- What are the implications of what we know and don't know? (These conclusions are your opinions, drawn from the facts.)
- What do we predict may happen? (Since you don't know what will happen, lay out possible scenarios – most likely, optimistic, pessimistic.)
- What resources and capabilities do we have at our disposal? Gaps? (These are your assets, both already deployed and available to be deployed, as well as holes you need to fill.)
- What aspects of the situation can we turn to our advantage? (This gets at resources that can be reallocated from other parts of your organization or other organizations, or opportunities created by the crisis. Look back at the organization's purpose for guidance here.)

[If managing virtually, document and distribute current best thinking. Team members provide an itemized response: 1) Questions for clarification; 2) What makes sense/keep, 3) Suggestions for improvement. Team decides what to keep and change.]

ALIGN ON SITUATIONAL OBJECTIVES AND INTENT:

This is about defining what is required to bridge the gap between the desired and most recent current state. "Intent" gets at why that's important. For example, when a glass water bottle capper went bad, grinding screw top threads into glass chips, the objective and intent were 1) stop the damage and 2) protect the brand.

PREPARE COMMUNICATION:

- Agree Organizing Concept (The core strategic idea to communicate flowing from objectives and intent.)
- Agree three main communication points.
- Communicate emotionally, rationally and inspirationally

SET TACTICAL PRIORITIES:

Be clear on whether the priorities cut across all scenarios or whether they are options to pursue depending upon which scenario unfolds.

Each priority needs a single, accountable leader. Lay out and implement the actions for each priority, with timing and a single, accountable leader for each action. As you get new information, your tactical priorities may change, leadership should not.

Priority: _____ Leader: _____

    Actions: _____ When: _____ Who: _____ Status: _____

    Actions: _____ When: _____ Who: _____ Status: _____

    Actions: _____ When: _____ Who: _____ Status: _____

AGREE PROTOCOLS:

- Clarify what tactical decisions people can make on their own vs. escalate
- Define and communicate exactly how the everyone should deal with surprises
- To make sure information moves accurately and quickly, the following meetings are mandatory:

MEETINGS:

Daily

1. Team has a 5-15-minute huddle first thing every morning (live or virtually)

   - Team leaders shares any updates to Context, Objectives, or Tactical Priorities
   - Each participant goes through wins, learning, help for their Tactical Priorities

     1. **Wins**—Share and celebrate the good things that have already happened
     2. **Learning**—Share learning that can help others
     3. **Help**—Highlight areas needing more support

2. Communication Lead sends an end of day email or video update to everyone.

----

3 – Bridge the long-term gaps.

Bridge the gaps between desired and current response and crisis prevention (improving things and reducing risks for the future).

At the end of the crisis, conduct an after-action review looking at:

- What actually happened? How did that compare with what we expected to happen?
- What impact did we have? How did that compare with our objectives?
- What did we do particularly effectively that we should do again?
- What can we do even better the next time in terms of risk mitigation and response?

This kicks off preparing in advance for the next crisis.

PART III Different Ownership Structures, Different Ground Rules

The BRAVE leadership framework includes tools to navigate strategic points of inflection in your business – for businesses of all sizes and in all industries. As leaders, the ownership structure of your business will sometimes create unique twists to consider in your BRAVE approach to your particular circumstances. As you look to transform an organization through a point of inflection, you will typically be time bound and have from a few months to a few years to make your impact. As you push for change, the ground rules for managing timing, setting investment levels, and communicating to key stakeholders will be different between public companies, private equity-backed businesses, and family-owned businesses.

As a leader in a public company, you may be building a company to create lasting value but you will be communicating with a large and engaged audience on a quarterly basis. Are you prepared to balance the long-term outlook required by inflection points with the short-term perspective of your investors and public markets?

As a leader in a private equity-backed business, you will have a compressed time frame to create value but also more latitude in your external communications without public market responsibility. Do you have a clear view of the appetite – and the expectations - of your owners as you execute your strategic plan?

As a leader in a family-owned business, you have a longer runway and a finite set of stakeholders to manage but also likely inherit a more conservative attitude toward growing the business. Will you have the financial and emotional support required to navigate a turning point in your business?

As you consider these BRAVE twists for your situation, let's refresh on the components of the BRAVE leadership framework:

- **E**nvironment: clarify your situation and field of play
- **V**alues: Align all around the organization's mission, vision and guiding principles
- **A**ttitude: Make choices around overarching strategy, priorities and culture
- **R**elationships: the heart of leadership – connecting and communicating
- **B**ehaviors: Getting things done – action – impact – effect

BRAVE Leadership Twists: Public Companies

Public investors will react to the promise of a strong vision – your story to navigate a point of inflection - and then hold you accountable on a quarterly basis to do what you said you were going to do. Consider these BRAVE twists for your situation:

> BRAVE Twist on Attitude: Your Competitors and Strategy as a Public Company

> Be attuned to your competition as you communicate your strategy. Public markets will shine a light on you alongside your competitors and you will be linked whether you like it or not. Particularly if your story is in response to your competitor's position – or their disruption of your business – you will be judged on the viability of your new strategic direction and there will be a premium on demonstrating that action and substance accompanies your words.

> BRAVE Twist on Relationships: Communicating with External Stakeholders as a Public Company

> Your communications with external stakeholders become public record in many cases as a public company. Finding the right balance of transparency with deliberate and purposeful communication can be challenging. Refine your story for change, tell that story consistently – and repeatedly – across internal and external audiences, and be measured in your progress updates in order to deliver consistent statements of progress as you navigate change. Being 'on message' consistently, and not delivering negative surprises, will build respect and trust in your audience – both internally and externally.

> It cannot be stated more bluntly: your consistency in delivering on your commitments is most important – a series of positive quarters where you deliver what you said you would do is more important than one splashy quarterly announcement.\

BRAVE Twist on Behaviors: Action Shouldn't Wait For The Next Earnings Call

The quarterly cadence of earnings calls for a public company can sometimes create a significant burst of energy in the few weeks before each call. The energy is entirely focused on packaging a positive story around the results of the prior three months since the last call. Often times, the end of the earnings call creates a week of executive management 'exhale' as the team recovers from that burst of energy.

There is no time to relax. The energy that you put into executing during the first few weeks of every quarter is much more impactful to your next earnings call than is the last few weeks of polishing your message before that next call. Your story on each earnings call will have much more substance if you focus on early execution more than last minute story polishing.

BRAVE Leadership Twists: Public Companies
- o **E**nvironment: Clarify your situation and field of play
- o **V**alues: Align all around the organization's mission, vision and guiding principles
- o **A**ttitude: Make choices around overarching strategy, priorities and culture
    - ▪ Pay particular attention to your sustainable competitive advantages vis a vis competitors
- o **R**elationships: The heart of leadership – connecting and communicating
    - ▪ Pay particular attention to communication with external stakeholders
- o **B**ehaviors: Getting things done – action – impact – effect
    - ▪ Yes. Quarterly earnings calls matters. But get ahead of them by managing the first few weeks of every quarter and not just the last days.

BRAVE Leadership Twists: Private Equity-backed Companies

Private equity (PE) ownership can create great opportunities for leadership teams to create significant value creation in a business over a finite period. In fact, every new PE ownership situation is most likely intended to create a point of inflection in order to materially change the growth trajectory of the business. Typically, your business will experience a "J Curve" where upfront investments and management fees will lead to a short-term dip in business valuation in order to create a financial inflection point and grow the company at a faster rate as the investment pays dividends.

Of course, the great opportunity to create value is also accompanied by expectations. Consider these BRAVE twists for your situation:

BRAVE Twist on Environment: Fully Understand Your PE Situation

There is a premium on understanding your situation when taking a leadership role with a private equity-owned business. Do your diligence on ownership time horizons for typical portfolio companies and the expected life of the fund. Understand the financial model that the PE firm used to sell the investment to their investment committee – you should be comfortable that the growth expectations are realistic. Ensure that you have a clear view of the inhibitors to growth – whether they be secular change, competitive changes, or customer dynamics – as these can sometimes be blind spots to aggressive financial investors.

BRAVE Twist on Attitude: Understand Your Levers For Investment

Your strategy may depend upon the level and type of investment provided by your PE owners. Your early days with this new ownership situation are no time to be shy about obtaining financial support in the context of your investors' bias to organic growth versus acquisitions, and their appetite for investment in physical, technical and human infrastructure.

Understand your levers for investment and how those investments will impact the financial metrics that are most important to your investors …and aggressively utilize those levers. Creating an inflection point on your revenue curve requires bold action.

BRAVE Twist on Relationships: Communicate More Than Board Meetings Require

You are partners with your private equity owners and transparency in communicating is vital. While you will have formal board meetings (likely quarterly,) you must find a communication cadence that is much more frequent with your PE board members. The momentum that you build via regular communication with your PE team will pay off in the trust and openness in your relationship. Trust will allow you to navigate business challenges with a 'benefit of the doubt' that will help you handle tough situations without worrying about the reaction of your board at the next board meeting.

Be on the lookout for shadow board members, not formally on the board, but voting through proxies. These may include senior members of investing PE firms shepherding the deal and venture without formal seats on the board. You'll want to include them in your communication efforts.

BRAVE Twist on Behaviors: Refining Ideas Into Actions

One positive benefit of open communication with a team of smart financial investors is that it can lead to a healthy flow of ideas. It can also lead to an unhealthy flow of ideas. That's right, you will find this a tricky balance. The inevitable flow of ideas can make it challenging for you to keep your team focused on strategic priorities.

Your owners mean well and have a vested interest in your success. Be open and receptive to the ideas coming from your board and keep them engaged in thinking about your business. That said, be selective in choosing those ideas that are worthy of your team being distracted from their core mission. You want an engaged board and you want a focused team – it's on you to get both.

<u>BRAVE Leadership Twists: Private Equity-backed Companies</u>
- o **E**nvironment: Clarify your situation and field of play
  - ▪ Fully understand your PE situation – and especially the time horizon of the applicable fund.
- o **V**alues: Align all around the organization's mission, vision and guiding principles
- o **A**ttitude: Make choices around overarching strategy, priorities and culture
  - ▪ Pay particular attention to your levers for investment across organic growth, acquisitions, physical, technical and human infrastructure.
- o **R**elationships: The heart of leadership – connecting and communicating
  - ▪ Be transparent in regular communication with all the key PE stakeholders including board members, shadow board members and those supporting and influencing them.
- o **B**ehaviors: Getting things done – action – impact – effect
  - ▪ Don't confuse ideas with priorities. Filter the best ideas from all involved into the few most important action priorities at any time.

BRAVE Leadership Twists: Family-owned Companies

Family-owned companies can often create brands, culture, and employee engagement that attract customers and employees to the values of the company. Family owners, though, are truly spending their own money to invest in change or navigate strategic points of inflection for the company. Be realistic about navigating your point of inflection and consider these BRAVE twists for your situation:

BRAVE Twist on Environment: Family Legacies Are At Stake

Choosing the right field of play is key to creating a turning point for your family-owned business. Are you entirely sure that your view of the business challenge, and your vision for a new direction, are completely in sync with the mind of the person whose name is attached to this business? Beyond the fact that you are intending to use their cash to pursue any new direction, their family legacy is dependent upon your changes. Put yourself in their shoes, your plan must thoughtfully understand the balance of risk and reward for these families who don't have much of a wall built between their personal lives and their business lives.

BRAVE Twist on Values: Don't Be Fooled Into Thinking Only One Person Matters

There is no doubt that you likely have one family member who matters a lot more than everyone else. Take care of that one person but also realize that you will want to touch base with all the family members that are active with this business, some of which may have a different last name and some of which may not even work for the organization! Family influences and opinions will impact your 'most important person' and you will be well served to understand the power base of the family and how family politics spill over into family business.

BRAVE Leadership Twists: Family-owned Companies
- o **E**nvironment: Clarify your situation and field of play
  - ▪ Be cognizant of the family's legacy.
- o **V**alues: Align all around the organization's mission, vision and guiding principles
  - ▪ In this case "all" means all those family members active and influencing the business whatever their last name happens to be.
- o **A**ttitude: Make choices around overarching strategy, priorities and culture
  - ▪ Pay particular attention to your levers for investment across organic growth, acquisitions, physical, technical and human infrastructure.
- o **R**elationships: The heart of leadership – connecting and communicating
  - ▪ Be transparent in regular communication with all the key PE stakeholders including board members, shadow board members and those supporting and influencing them.
- o **B**ehaviors: Getting things done – action – impact – effect
  - ▪ Don't confuse ideas with priorities. Filter the best ideas from all involved into the few most important action priorities at any time.

Regardless of your owners, your stakeholders, your financial reporting responsibilities, or your company size, what matters most in your career is your reputation. Your reputation will outlast your last quarter, your last investment, your last deal opportunity, even your last job. Your character during times of change will determine how people remember you. Those people may be your next board member, your next private equity owner, a future business partner, or the faithful employees that will follow you on your next challenge. Be a good person. Be fair. Be strong and open in the face of difficult decisions. You own your reputation so take good care of it.

With all that in mind accelerate through a point of inflection by deploying five overlapping steps or building blocks differently in different situations:

Assess & Plan	Strategy	Organization	Operations
Change catalysts:	Overarching strategy	Future capability plan	Leadership approach
Situation/ambitions	Strategic priorities	Immediate role sort	Management cadence
Best Current Thinking	Cultural changes	Leadership mindset	Incentives
Ongoing purpose-driven **learning & communication**			

- **Assess** changes in your situation/environment or ambitions/values, SWOT, 5Cs and Shared Purpose.
- Relook at your **strategy**/attitude and how to win at a particular point on Porter's value chain, digging into Bassat's for whom, what, who, with what, where, and when model, finding the most valuable niche, aligning your culture and creating a plan.
- Get your **organization** and team relationships right with a future-proofed ADEPT team focused on SMARTER goals.
- Set **operations** with the right behaviors across innovation, your management cadence, milestone management and creative briefs.
- Lead with ongoing purpose-driven **communication** through message, amplifiers and perseverance internally and externally.

Focus more on different BRAVE tools in different situations like a full transformational change, facing a particular competitive challenge, a new private equity owner, a push for organic growth, or integrating a merger or acquisition as laid out below.

Application of BRAVE Tools in Different Situations

Transformational Change (Full suite of tools)

- Environment:
    - SWOT Exercise (Strengths, Weaknesses, Opportunities, Threats)
    - 5Cs Exercise (Customers, Collaborators, Capabilities, Competitors, Conditions)
- Values:
    - Shared Purpose Modeling (Mission, Vision, Values Guiding Principles)
- Attitudes:
    - Porter Value Chain Model (Design, Produce, Deliver, Service)
    - Ben Bassat's W6 (For whom, what, who, with what, where, when)
    - Finding Niches via 5Cs
    - BRAVE Cultural Mapping
    - 6-Step Strategic Plan
- Relationships:
    - MAP (Message – Amplifiers – Perseverance)
    - People Management Tools
    - ADEPT team building (Acquire, Develop, Encourage, Plan, Transition)
    - SMARTER Goal Setting (Specific, Measurable, Actionable/Attainable, Relevant, Time bound, Encouraging/Exciting, Rewarded)
    - Communication Planning
    - Press Interview Management as appropriate
- Behaviors:
    - BRAVE Innovation
    - BRAVE Management Cadence (Priorities, Programs, Projects, Tasks)
    - BRAVE Milestone Management (What, When, Who)
    - BRAVE Creative Briefs

Competitive Challenges (Focus areas)

- Environment:
    - SWOT Exercise
    - 5Cs Exercise
- Values:
    - Shared Purpose Modeling
- Attitudes:
    - Porter Value Chain Model
    - Ben Bassat's W6
    - Finding Niches via 5Cs
    - 6-Step Strategic Plan
- Relationships:
    - MAP (Message – Amplifiers – Perseverance)
    - ADEPT team building
    - SMARTER Goal Setting
- Behaviors:
    - BRAVE Innovation

New Private Equity Owner (Focus areas)

- Environment:
    - SWOT Exercise
    - 5Cs Exercise
- Values:
    - Shared Purpose Modeling
- Attitudes:
    - 6-Step Strategic Plan
- Relationships:
    - MAP (Message – Amplifiers – Perseverance)
    - People Management Tools
    - ADEPT team building
    - SMARTER Goal Setting
    - Communication Planning
- Behaviors:
    - BRAVE Management Cadence
    - BRAVE Milestone Management

Organic Growth Push (Focus Areas)

- Environment:
    - SWOT Exercise
    - 5Cs Exercise
- Values:
    - Shared Purpose Modeling
- Attitudes:
    - Ben Bassat's W6
    - Finding Niches via 5Cs
    - 6-Step Strategic Plan
- Relationships:
    - MAP (Message – Amplifiers – Perseverance)
    - ADEPT team building
    - SMARTER Goal Setting
    - Communication Planning
- Behaviors:
    - BRAVE Management Cadence
    - BRAVE Milestone Management

Merger and Acquisition Integration (Focus Areas)

- Environment:
    - SWOT Exercise
- Values:
    - Shared Purpose Modeling
- Attitudes:
    - BRAVE Cultural Mapping
- Relationships:
    - MAP (Message – Amplifiers – Perseverance)
    - ADEPT team building
    - SMARTER Goal Setting
    - Communication Planning
    - Press Interview Management as appropriate
- Behaviors:
    - BRAVE Milestone Management
    - BRAVE Creative Briefs

Final thoughts

Brave leadership is about inspiring, enabling and empowering others to do their absolute best together to realize a meaningful and rewarding shared purpose.

So, in leading through a point of inflection, be good and brave. Be other-focused and leverage the BRAVE framework to help others be who they should be, say what they should say and get done what they need to get done, thinking in terms of:

- Where to play?
- What matters and why?
- How to win?
- How to connect?
- What impact?

Appendix I: Looking Across the Four Cores

We propose four primary areas of focus: design, produce, deliver, and service. The choice of which of those areas on which to focus dictates your organizational and operational choices. This note looks at each one in turn.

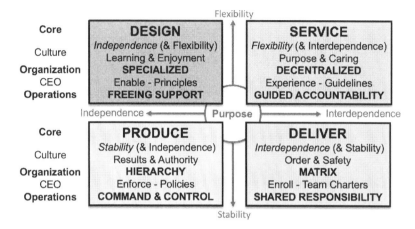

Value is defined as the customer's view of the relation between your perceived, relative benefits and your perceived, relative costs.

- Design-focused organizations win by imagining new valuable things.
- Production-focused organizations win by making valuable things out of disparate elements.
- Delivery-focused organizations win by conveying valuable things from one party to another.
- Service-focused organizations win by valuably enhancing their customers' experiences.

While most organizations do some level of design, production, delivery and service, and all must market and sell, the most successful organizations have a clear focus on one of the first four areas.

***** Design *****

To focus on design is create, adapt or arrange something new.

- Create things that did not exist before and are new to the world.
- Adapt things that did exist, modifying them to make them fit for a new use.
- Arrange things by putting them into "proper order or into a correct or suitable sequence, relationship or adjustment" so the new whole is greater than the sum of the parts.

Design Culture A design-focused organization's main cultural driver should be independence. Its designers should feel free to get their inspiration from anywhere they can. Flexibility, learning and enjoyment support that. But independence rules.

Specialized Organizations work especially well in design-focused organizations. Designers and inventors have special and often rare strengths. The rest of the organization has to nurture and protect them, minimizing unproductive distractions so they can spend their time creating, adapting and arranging.

CEO as Chief Enabler

In an organization basing its success on its ability to nurture and protect its designers, the CEO has to be the chief enabler. Great leaders bring out others self-confidence. They do this in large part by emphasizing confidence-building in their approach to the direction, authority, resource, and accountability aspects of delegation. This is especially important when it comes to designers.

Direction

Emphasize the problem you need solved or the opportunity you can take advantage of. Then, give them as much freedom as you can about how they solve it. The more they can think with the mind of a child, the better.

Authority

Give them the authority to experiment. By definition, the "new" won't match what you currently have and do. Not the authority to experiment is not the authority to implement.

Resources

This one is counter-intuitive but <u>adding constraints increases innovation</u>. Think in terms of scope, time and resource constrained creative sprints instead of never-ending quests.

Accountability

The key here is assuming success. Have confidence in your designers. Recognize and reward them for their achievements at the end of creative sprints along the way to bring out their self-confidence.

Operate with Freeing Support

Design behavior is fragile. All need to give it freeing support to keep it going. <u>The ABCs of changing behavior</u> apply.

The antecedent is prompting designers to create, adapt and arrange as part of your approach to delegation. Assuming you've got the right people with the right direction and support, they are likely to do what you asked them to do.

The trap here is consequences, and especially unintended negative consequences of positive behavior. Make sure you and everyone interacting with your designers are:

- Positively reinforcing desired behavior (creating, adapting, arranging.)
- Punishing undesirable behavior (outside acceptable norms.)

Change the way you:

- Positively reinforce undesirable behavior
- Punish desired behavior (by applying others' standards to their output.)

You may have success by leading with principles (as opposed to more rigid policies or more directional guidelines.) Principles help people come to their own decisions in a way that fits your vision and values.

To focus on production is to create a competitive advantage in reliably and repeatedly bringing disparate elements together into something with more value.

Production Culture A production-focused organization's main cultural driver should be stability. People should know what they are expected to do and get it done consistently and reliably. While that suggests a degree of independence and there should be a clear focus on results and respect for authority, stability rules.

Hierarchical Organizations work especially well in production-focused organizations. Production is all about bringing disparate elements together. Individual performers should follow the direction of first-line supervisors in working on their pieces. Those higher and higher in the hierarchy will have broader and broader views of how things fit to optimized how they are all pulled together.

CEO as Chief Enforcer

In an organization basing its success on its ability to produce reliably and consistently, the CEO should be the chief enforcer. If everyone is looking up in a hierarchy, they are ultimately looking up at the CEO. Any wobble there can destabilize everyone in the hierarchy below the CEO – which is everyone.

Lead with policies mandating definite courses or methods of action that all must follow.

- Policy: mandatory, definite course of method of action that all must follow.
- Guidelines: preferred course or method of action that all should generally follow.
- Principles – ways of thinking about action

Operate with Command and Control For production-focused organizations, policies inspire, enable and empower. Producers find clarity inspiring. Tight swim lanes enable them to do their job.

Swim Lanes

- Producers work best with swim lanes separated by solid walls topped with barbed wire.
- Deliverers working across a matrix want to know where various players' swim lanes intersect.
- Servers focused on customer experience need flexible swim lanes so they can go wherever required to satisfy their customers.
- Designers and inventors don't even want to be told they have to swim, let alone have swim lanes.

Producers love enforcers. Others in the organization won't be so sure. Those that value independence will see the organization as too controlling. Those that value flexibility will see the organization as too rigid.

If you're leading producers, be unapologetic about your policies and controls. Those that choose not to follow those policies and live with those controls should choose to work elsewhere. Or you should make that choice for them. The #1 regret experienced leaders have looking back on their careers is not moving fast enough on people. In a hierarchy, people will look to the leader for examples of leadership. In these cases, some early public hangings can send exactly the right signals to those looking for stability and clarity.

***** Deliver *****

To focus on delivery is to build a competitive advantage in conveying valuable things from one person, place or thing to another. SIPOC helps (Supplier, Input, Process, Output, Customer):

- Your **Supplier** (person, place or thing) supplies you with
- The **Input** (what you will deliver) which you run through your
- Delivery/distribution/conveyance **Process** to get
- The **Output** (what you will deliver) to
- Your **Customer**.

Note the input and output are the same. You're not involved in design – imagining valuable things. You don't produce – making valuable things out of disparate elements. And you don't do after sale/after delivery service. Of course, delivery is a service itself. But your focus is on conveying your input safer, faster and less expensive than others - not on the experience of the people or things you are conveying. That's the fundamental strategic choice guiding your allocation of resources.

Delivery Culture. A delivery-focused organization's main cultural driver should be interdependence. Its people should think eco-system first and ask how to make the system work better at every chance they get. Stability, order and safety matter on the way to creating scalable, repeatable processes. But interdependence and connections rule.

Matrix Organization. Matrix organizations work especially well in delivery-focused organizations. This forces the supplier and customer-focused groups within the organization to work with the functionally-focused groups. Matrices work when everyone buys into shared objectives and goals and fail when people try to protect their own turf first.

CEO as Chief Enroller. In an organization basing its success on its ability to enroll suppliers, allies and customers and clients that can benefit from each other's offerings, the CEO has to be the chief enroller. The CEO's job is to bring people into the ecosystem and get them to collaborate with each other.

Operate with Shared Responsibilities. Delivery-focused organizations succeed only when people accept shared responsibilities. They live in the world of hand-offs. Things have to be ready to go when people are ready to pick them up. People have to be ready to pick things up when they are ready to go. Shared responsibilities.

The main trap for delivery organizations is diversification. Many get fooled into thinking they can create more value and make more money by dialing up their services. The U-Shaped profit curve rules. Supermarkets deliver large quantities of acceptable flowers to their customers at relatively low prices. Flowerbx delivers smaller quantities of near-perfect flowers at relatively high prices. They both win. Hallmark tried to charge higher prices for barely acceptable flowers and lost.

Know what you do. Know where you play on the U-Shaped profit curve. Focus to win. Or dilute your efforts and lose.

Team charters are especially useful in matrix organizations. Use them to get team members aligned around their purpose, objectives, context, approach, guidelines and implementation accountabilities.

***** Experience *****

Service is ultimately about how you make your customers feel. Design, production and delivery matter. But they only matter as platforms on which to build the experience.

Service Culture. A service-focused organization's main cultural driver should be flexibility. The front-line people interacting with customers must have the flexibility to meet their needs and exceed their expectations on the spot. Interdependence matters because the front-line people will need to leverage the rest of the organization to help customers. Purpose and caring matter a great deal in uniting all around customer service. But flexibility should rule.

Decentralized Organizations work especially well in service-focused organizations. This is inextricably linked to flexibility. Drive decision-making as close to the customer as possible.

The fundamental difference between a decentralized organization and a matrix organization is control of resource allocation decisions. In a matrix organization the geographic or customer-facing people share decisions with functional leaders. E.g. the Florida state manager and national marketing manager must agree on the Florida advertising spend. In a decentralized organization, the geographic or customer-facing people make their own decisions, like the Florida advertising spend.

This makes for faster, more flexible, more customer-experience focused decisions.

CEO as Chief Experience Officer. In an organization basing its success on its ability to create superior experiences for its customers, the CEO has to be the Chief Experience Officer. The Chief Experience Officer owns the vision and the values. They must live customer experience in everything they say, do, and are. If they don't fundamentally believe, they will get caught.

Just as Ben Hunt-Davis and his teammates evaluated every choice with the question, "Will it make the boat go faster?" on their way to Olympic Rowing Gold in 2000, the Chief Experience Officer should evaluate every choice with the question, "Will it improve customers' experience?"

Operate with Guided Accountability. Great customer service organizations operate with guided accountable. Everyone holds themselves accountable for how they make each and every customer they come in contact with feel.

Clear guidelines are critical. Think Goldilocks. Policies - mandatory, definite courses of action that all must follow - are too strict. Principles – ways of thinking about action – are too loose. Guidelines – preferred courses or methods of action that all should generally follow – are just right, freeing people up to act in the best interest of the customer with the guidance they need to make decisions on the spot.

If you're leading a service organization, both parts of guided accountability are critical to effective decentralization. Decentralizing without guidance is abrogating your authority. Guidance without accountability turns the guidance into theoretical gibberish. Only by letting people take up true accountability for the customer experience within agreed guidelines will things go the way you want. Though, if you've read this far you know that it's not about what you want. It's about what the customer wants.

Appendix II: Virtual Meeting/Workshop Management

We are social beings. We meet to share knowledge, to work together & build relationships, and to make decisions & drive to action. Others will comply with decisions if they are made aware, even indirectly. To contribute, they need to understand through direct communication. But if you want them to commit, they have to believe in each other and in the decisions, requiring connecting emotionally.

Words on paper, emails, messages and other platforms are generally sufficient to share knowledge.

Voice communication adds tone to the words, improving the quality of working together.

Live meetings are best for building relationships, emotional connections, and commitment to decisions as people breath the same air and communicate with words, tone and body language.

The urgent need for social distancing in light of the spread of COVID-19, creates a need to get as much of the benefit of live meetings as we can without people breathing the same air and coming into physical contact. Virtual meetings via video, webinars, web conferencing, or virtual worlds can get us there with increased attention and investment in preparation, delivery, and follow through including:

- **More deliberate content and flow planning** because it's harder to adjust on the fly.
- **A different approach to delivery**, doing more work before and after the meetings themselves, and switching between technological platforms instead of physical spaces to revitalize attention.
- **More, better, and stronger meeting facilitation** given the process complexities to allow leaders and participants to keep their focus on relationships and content.

General Approach

PREPARATION: Set overall single objective and clear expectations for knowledge-sharing, working together, relationship-building, and decision-making by agenda item and attendee in line with that single objective; and make sure to get appropriate pre-work and pre-reading to people far enough in advance for all to learn/contribute to their fullest potential. [Same for live and virtual meetings]

DELIVERY: Manage meeting participation and timing to optimize knowledge sharing, collaboration, relationship-building, decisions – perhaps with Best Current Thinking Problem (BCT) Solving process.

- Virtual **knowledge sharing** via webinars or virtual world rooms – one way with Q&A

- Virtual **working together & relationship-building** via problem solving approach below

- Virtual **decision-making** via small group video conferences or virtual rooms (5-9 people)

FOLLOW THROUGH: Get meeting notes out promptly to memorialize decisions and actions, kicking off the preparation for the next meeting.

Problem-Solving Approach

1. In the beginning, there is a problem. Identify the problem owner and decision maker who may or may not be different people. Decide whether to work the problem as a group (or not.) If yes,

2. The problem owner shares the going-in perspective on the problem, context, and Best Current Thinking around potential options. (Ideally shared before the problem-solving session.) [Virtually in first webinar or virtual meeting room]

3. Answer questions for clarification (to help people understand context and Best Current Thinking, not for them to comment on or improve the thinking – yet.) [Virtually in chat box in first webinar]

4. Highlight the most positive of the Best Current Thinking contributing to making it work. [Virtually via chat box in first webinar]

5. Identify the key barriers keeping the Best Current Thinking from working. (Get all the barriers on the table at the same time before working any of them.) [Virtually via chat box in first webinar]

6. Decide on the most important barrier. [Virtually problem owner's choice after first webinar]]

7. Directed brainstorm on the most important barrier: WYDIS (What You Do Is) with all participating, including the problem owner – generally need 6-8 WYDIS. [Virtually via open chat room or virtual team room for a day or two]

8. Problem owner pulls together into a possible remedy to that barrier (testing.) [Virtually problem owner regroups.]

9. If the possible remedy is not strong enough, continue to work this barrier. If the remedy works, determine whether that is enough to solve the overall problem. If yes, move on to action steps. If not, work the next most important barrier. [Virtually via second webinar or virtual team room session]

10. Action Steps: Agree what will get done by when by whom now that this problem is solved. [Virtually via small group video call or meeting in virtual team room]

About the authors

George Bradt has led the revolution in how people start new jobs - accelerating transitions so leaders and their teams reduce their rates of failure and fulfill potential. After Harvard and Wharton (MBA), he progressed through sales, marketing, and general management roles around the world at Unilever, Procter & Gamble, Coca-Cola, and J.D. Power's Power Information Network spin off as chief executive. Now he is Chairman of PrimeGenesis, author of 10 books on onboarding and leadership, 700+ columns for Forbes, and eighteen plays and musicals (book, lyrics & music).

Onboarding books authored or co-authored by George Bradt:
- Point of Inflection (GHP Press 2017-20)
- The New Leader's 100-Day Action Plan (John Wiley & Sons, 2006, 2009, 2011, 2016)
- First-Time Leader (John Wiley & Sons, 2014)
- The New Job 100-Day Plan (GHP Press, 2012)
- The New Leader's Playbook (GHP Press, one/year 2011-2019)
- The Total Onboarding Program: An Integrated Approach (Wiley/Pfeiffer, 2010)
- Onboarding: How to Get Your New Employees up to Speed in Half the Time (John Wiley & Sons, 2009)
- Influence and Impact (John Wiley & Sons, 2021)

George can be reached at gbradt@primegenesis.com

Jeff Scott has been a proven transformational leader in the information and media industry for 20 years as a CTO, COO, President, and CEO. With roots in digital product development, Jeff has led businesses ranging from small, private-equity-backed enterprises to large information companies and found himself at the forefront of many technology and business evolutions. A common thread in all of those businesses were the strategic inflection points and complex transitions that honed his appreciation for the value of leadership in times of transformational change.

Jeff can be reached at jscott@primegenesis.com.

References

Bradt, George. 2011–2020 *The New Leader's Playbook*. Articles on Forbes.com.

Bradt, George, Jayme Check, and John Lawler. 2016. *The New Leader's 100-Day Action Plan*. 4th ed. Hoboken, NJ: John Wiley & Sons.

Bradt, George, and Gillian Davis. 2014. *First-Time Leader*. Hoboken, N: John Wiley & Sons

Bradt, George, and Ed Bancroft. 2010. *The Total Onboarding Program*. San Francisco: Wiley/Pfeifer.

Bradt, George, and Mary Vonnegut. 2009. *Onboarding: How to Get Your New Employees up to Speed in Half the Time*. Hoboken, NJ: John Wiley & Sons.

Bradt, George, and Mary Vonnegut. 2012. *The New Job 100-Day Plan*. New York: PrimeGenesis.

Buckingham, Marcus, and Donald Clifton. 2001. *Now Discover Your Strengths*. New York: Free Press.

Campbell, Joseph. 1949. *The Hero with a Thousand Faces*. New York: Pantheon.

Covey, Steven. 1989. *The 7 Habits of Highly Effective People*. New York: Simon & Schuster

Coyne, Kevin P., and Edward J. Coyne. 2007 "Surviving Your New CEO." *Harvard Business Review*, May.

Doran, G. T. 1981. "There's a S.M.A.R.T. Way to Write Management's Goals and Objectives." Management Review 70, no. 11 (AMA Forum): 35–36.

Feldman, Mark I and Spratt, Michael F. 1998 *Five Frogs on a Log*. New York. Harpers Business.

Fisher, Anne. 2012. "New Job? Get a Head Start Now." *Fortune*, February

Groysberg, Boris, Andrew Hill, and Toby Johnson. 2010. "Which of These People Is Your Future CEO?" *Harvard Business Review*, November.

Harrald, John. 2006. "Agility and Discipline: Critical Success Factors for Disaster Response." *The ANNALS of the American Academy of Political and Social Science* 604: 256.

Heiman, Stephen, and Diane Sanchez. 1998. *The New Strategic Selling*. New York: Warner Books.

Hsieh, Tony. 2012. *Delivering Happiness: A Path to Profits, Passion, and Purpose*. Mundelein, IL: Round Table Comics.

Linver, Sandy. 1994. *Speak and Get Results*. New York: Simon & Schuster.

Lodish, Leonard. 1984. Class discussion.: University of Pennsylvania, Wharton School

McDermott, Meaghan M. 2008. "Brizard Takes City School District's Reins Today." *Rochester Democrat and Chronicle*, January 2.

Schein, Edgar. 1985. *Organizational Culture and Leadership*. San Francisco: Jossey-Bass.

Senge, Peter, Art Kleiner, Charlotte Roberts, Richard Ross, and Bryan Smith. 1994. *The Fifth Discipline Fieldbook*. London: Nicholas Brealey Publishing.

Smith, Bruay. 1994. *The Fifth Discipline Field Book*. Boston: Nicholas Brealey. Publishing.

Walker, Sam. 2018 *The Captain Class; The Hidden Force Behind The World's Greatest Teams*. New York: Random House

Note: The tools printed in this book are also available in a customizable format at www.onboardingtools.com. (See the BRAVE Leadership page.) We will be regularly updating these tools and adding videos and additional material on that page to give you the benefit of our latest thinking.